TESTIMONIALS

"Life is not the opposite of death. It is birth and death that are opposites. Life is the continuum of birth and death eternally, and now.
Read this engrossing book for your own insights into reality."
Deepak Chopra, M.D.
Best-Selling Author, *Life After Death: The Burden of Proof*

"A stunning book! *Light in the Mourning* is filled with compelling stories that grabbed my heart and transformed me inside and out.
Thank you, Margo, for the gift of this beautiful and life-changing book."
Marci Shimoff
International Speaker
#1 *NY Times* Bestselling Author,
Happy for No Reason, Love for No Reason, Chicken Soup for the Woman's Soul

"Reading Margo Lenmark's book, *Light in the Mourning*, was a truly fascinating, mind-opening, heart-expanding and thoroughly entertaining experience! Margo is a marvelously gifted and courageous story teller with so much wit, wisdom, and passion that each chapter held me totally captivated.

"I believe this to be an extraordinary book with the power to truly nourish the soul, soothe the heart and guide the mind into a deeper and more reverent understanding of our uniquely sacred human journey. I wholeheartedly recommend it!"
Sergio Baroni
LCSW, Psychotherapist in private practice.

"The subject of death, especially in The United States, lays in a wasteland of denial.

"When I met Margo Lenmark, I immediately recognized her as an important "outlier" on the subject of death and dying. Rather than coming from just a scientific discipline, Margo's "second sight" brings her stories a deeply needed authenticity that embraces all religions and spiritual practices.

"Ms. Lenmark is a woman of remarkable insight. This important book brings comfort to all those who have suffered loss. More importantly, her gift will give all of us an opportunity to face both life and death with hope and serenity."
Genie Appel-Cohen
Artist/Educator

"Everyone should read this book unless you don't plan on dying. It brought me past all the petty stuff in my life. Every story is filled with unexpected wisdom that has opened my eyes to the beauty of death and even made me look forward to it. This book will speak to anyone."
Cynthia Swanson
Vice President/Owner, Arc Indexing Inc.

"As an oncologist, I deal with death daily. Personally, I recently lost both parents. Reading Margo's book was such an inspiration! She is so positive, and the lesson from the book is not only how to process the pain of losing a loved one but also direction in how to live our life. Love and forgiveness trump all. Read this book, and you will surely have a smile on your face and joy in your heart."
Yvonne Mack, M.D.
Radiation Oncologist

"I am personally very moved by this book.

"Margo Lenmark, with her book, *Light in the Mourning,* as the vehicle and guide, provides us with intimate and personal details about herself and important loved ones in her life. Her descriptions help us appreciate who she and they are and at the same time, we gain significant Universal and Spiritual knowledge about life and death.

"Her personal revelations took strong courage and deeply felt love so that others can better understand their relationships to loved ones and when these relationships transition from the living person to one who has passed away. She has given us a gift that has meaning in the present and can keep on giving. This is truly an act of love."

Barry Ostrow, M.D.
D.L.F.A.P.A, General Psychiatrist, Geriatric Psychiatrist, and Psychoanalyst

"*Light In The Mourning* is a fascinating insight into the emotional and spiritual revelations experienced by Margo through important relationships whom she has lost through death. It is through those who have touched us that we learn the true meaning of life, gifts they gave us and the path we choose to follow for our own peaceful, loving experience. Margo leads us through stories that help us in our own self-discoveries from those we have lost. Great book and a great experience for me reading it. Thank you."

Carolyn Holder
MA, LPC, Certified Thanatologist, Certified Grief Counselor

"Margo Lenmark grew up surrounded by death at the family funeral home. Still, no one is ready when death hits close to home. Finding herself besieged by death of friends and family members, Ms. Lenmark adapted and learned important life lessons deep in those shadows. Her radically transparent memoir exposes death of the body and sometimes of hope. Anyone facing or surviving the death of a loved one will garner great benefit from this read. Through her unique upbringing and perspective, she shines sunlight of hope. This book is a gift of an astute student of life. Profound spirituality, struggle, and insight make this author worth reading and sharing – more than once."
Dr. Wade E. Butler
Author, Hospice Care Counselor, and Spiritual Leader

Light
in the
Mourning

Memoirs of an Undertaker's Daughter

Margo Lenmark

There is no such thing as an ending...
just a place where you leave the story.
The Second Best Exotic Marigold Hotel

To my family.
Those who have left the story and those who have not.

ACKNOWLEDGMENTS

They say it takes a village and you'd think when writing your memoirs you could do it by yourself. But not so! Here is my village that helped make this book happen and who I wish to thank from the bottom of my heart.

First and foremost: Steve Berndt, Carol Hancock, Genie Cohen and Judi Beck. Your editing, feedback, and support absolutely propelled my book forward.

Close behind: Kim Betz, Mary Horak, Britannia Tomlinson, Anne Rasheed, and Donna Sechriest.

My actual village: Mark and Marty Lenmark, Mark's wife Judy without whose memory we wouldn't remember anything (!), Carmen Lenmark, and all my cousins, especially Hank and Buzzy Alexander for the memories and stories they shared while writing this.

I thank the following people who offered support over the 11 years it took to finish this book: Dave Linse, Carolyn Weaver, Andy and Betty Bargerstock, Debra Helene, Linda Hartnett, Jane Meyers, Patti Jupiter, Cyndy Hughes, Amy Laderoute, Debbie Arnold, Rob and Donna Glazier, Kathleen Deyo, Vickie Morse, Nancy Zetterval, Cynthia and Robert Swanson, Maggie and Elicka Peterson Sparks, Ken Laderoute, Amshiva Mallani, Peach Beckley, Tony DiRusso, Julia Kent, Wade Butler, Dana Willett and Dean Draznin. A special appreciation for Brian Bement who recently passed on. His eloquent words to me just before he died were in praise of my father and went straight into this book. Rest in peace, my friend.

Big thanks to Frank Walters Clark whose guidance every step of the way was invaluable and who helped me keep my voice through all the editing.

And finally, I thank Ellen Reifslager who made me promise to write a book about my father 20 years ago. A promise I never forgot and without which I would never have had the thought.

My love to all of you for the role you played in bringing this book to fruition and the beautiful role you play in my life.

CONTENTS

INTRODUCTION

Death will ever remain the great mystery that it is. But it has revealed to me very clear instructions about how to live. This is my account of how this wisdom was imparted and the indescribable gift that was given. It exposes the interwoven beauty between life and death and offers up the reason we need to grieve. This is as much a book about life as it is about death.

You never know what event in your life is going to change your life forever. Or when. And I can't tell you to be ready for it because you can't be. You can never prepare for the unexpected magnitude of such a destined occurrence.

In my life that event happened and everything I thought I knew ended in a flash. It was like the wind sheared my past life away and there was…nothing in my world…left. When my brother Mike died, a part of me did too. I found myself questioning all my answers. Every concept which held meaning suddenly vanished and I realized I knew nothing. So I promised myself that whatever came out of his death would become my living memorial to him.

Out of his ashes came this book.

Grief is the devastating aftermath of death. Most of us have to experience it many times during our lives, and it's a wonder we survive.

But for the passing soul, it is a different story.

I have had three near-death experiences in potential car accidents. In each one, the same thing happened. Each time, as the car swerved out of control, whether it was me driving or someone else, everything went into slow motion. It became calm and silent and clear, and not in the least bit anxious. For me, in that vast calm, it was a simple look at what was happening. I had plenty of time to evaluate all my options with no fear at all. I knew my soul would slip out without any pain to my body if the car were to crash because my soul was substantially separate from my body in that slow-motion experience. I believe that death happens in that same calmness in every circumstance no matter what the cause of death. I believe that is the ease with which the soul leaves the body at its moment of departure from this earth.

The days leading up to death may be difficult or tragic, but the actual experience is a moment in time. It is the greatest relief, and the biggest letting go that we will ever experience. It's the one event we have in common, yet most of us are afraid to address.

Perhaps because it is hidden away in our society or because it is out of the realm of our personal experience, we think of death as morbid or terrifying. But I don't think it is either of these for the one who is passing. I think it is an evolution of the soul and a beautiful one at that.

When the time comes to leave this physical world, I think it is going to be glorious beyond anything we can imagine. I believe it is so divinely orchestrated that when the time comes, we have no choice but to stop breathing and be embraced by the angels that brought us into this world.

Growing up around it in my father's funeral home made me

curious about the mysterious threshold between life and death and what happens when we die. When someone "passes on" where do they pass on to? Do they "go to heaven"? Do they go on living somewhere else in some other form? Are they here and we just can't see them? Do our loved ones live only in our hearts as a memory? People just disappear, so where do they go? And why? What's the point of it all?

So many unanswered questions.

I've had premonitions and cognitions throughout my life starting as a child. I often knew what was going to happen right before it happened. I would "see" someone was going to walk through the door and a minute later that person would walk through the door. One night our house burned down, and I had a premonition of the fire before falling asleep and cried myself to sleep not knowing what to do about it. Throughout my life, my friends would come over to talk to me about their problems, and I would "know" what was happening and explain it to them as if I had experienced it myself.

As I came face-to-face with the deaths of many loved ones, I had similar experiences during and after each loss. Each death shattered my paradigm like a rock in the windshield but left behind an important revelation about life. A specific message. It was like pulling back a curtain and seeing something in plain view. These unveilings are the most impressive gifts in my life as each was a total game changer for how I lived.

It has not been an easy ride. Death seems to blow my window wide open and expose things that I could never know any other way. This is my sojourn through many losses and the many lessons learned from them. It is my revelation about grief and why we need to do it. It is a thoughtful book. I invite you to sink deeply with me and engage in my journey, so you can vicariously "get" my same epiphanies.

I received these messages from the people I was grieving, as a sort of deathbed confession from them as to how to live life. But their wisdom is for everyone grieving or not.

I hope this book strengthens you, inspires you, and opens up fresh ways of seeing the world and the events that happen to us. If you are grieving, I hope this brings light to your mourning, and I stand with you in the presence of this greatest mystery.

We all have a window of perception through which we view the world, through which we try to understand it, through which we find our answers. Our windows are all different but all valid.

This book is mine.

THE FACE IN DEATH

I never feared my father's death.

I clutched my coat in the front of me and hunched forward for extra protection against the wind, but it couldn't protect me from the bitter chill in my psyche. My friend and I walked up the gradual incline of the sidewalk lined with crusty snow banks. At the top of the hill stood a 2-story building. The time-worn red brick with its white marble columns rose in sharp contrast to the snow-covered lawn. It stood there like a monument in the same understated regal sort of way that old money speaks over new.

It was bleak and overcast. We were exhausted having driven through ice storms to get here. The closer I got to the building, the more I was haunted by his warnings not to be here. Admonitions echoed through my head, but I reached for the long bronze handle on the heavy white door anyway and pulled it toward me.

Inside I was struck by the rich burgundy textures and gold ornamentation, tastefully reflecting the look of a bygone era. The room was filled with velvet Queen Anne chairs, polished wood, and thick floral brocade drapes. Over the white marble fireplace was a portrait of a distinguished man in a gray suit. The adjoining wall was adorned with three pictures of Jesus—one with folded hands, one praying in the garden of Gethsemane and one washing Mary's feet. There was an immense silence, a distinct smell of freshly cut flowers, and subdued light casting a pinkish glow in the room.

My mind raced with trepidation. Nothing in my life had caused such apprehension, yet I was gripped with determination to move forward.

We were greeted by a tall, elderly, soft-spoken gentleman with thick wavy hair; not one gray strand out of place. He was striking in his dark suit and crisp white shirt, but I noticed his collar was a little too tight causing small folds of skin to overlay the top edge. He reached for my hand in a show of both welcome and compassion. After taking our coats, he led us down a long, dark corridor to the rear of the building.

As we walked in silence, we stepped in unison with the antique clock that ticked quite loudly for such a quiet place. On the wall straight ahead was a picture of Jesus, his eyes following us all the way down the hallway. When we stopped, I noticed the floral aroma had faded to something less agreeable, something stale and musty. The kind man opened the door sending a waft of cool air our way. He stepped aside to allow us to enter first. An even colder chill ran through me as I stepped through the doorway and my eyes adjusted to the dim light of the room. Sheer emotion gripped my throat. I stood frozen in place. Stunned. I was mesmerized by what I saw. At the end of the room…this very long room was…my father.

I just stood there. Staring.

Absolutely nothing in the room was moving except the rise and fall of my chest. Not a sound except the beat of my heart. Nothing in my life had prepared me for this moment.

Something in that moment brought me back to an early childhood memory of my father. The last time I'd experienced this very same—very distinct—feeling was when I unexpectedly came upon him after church one

Sunday morning.

It was warm outside, so there was no need to run to the house to protect my young legs dangling from my Sunday school dress. My mom and brothers were close behind me as I opened the door. I started inside when what I saw stopped me dead in my tracks…

In the middle of the living room sat my father in his Sputnik patterned boxers, eyes closed, his legs crossed in the Indian style lotus position. He had a carrot in one hand and a tomato in the other, the sun streaming golden rays across his face. He looked like an ad in a yoga magazine. Utterly intrigued I stared in fascination. In a moment like this, breaking the silence is like dropping a pebble into a glassy-smooth pond. Nevertheless, I heard my five-year-old voice inquire, "Dad, what are you doing?" "Shhhh….I'm trying to reach Samadhi" he replied unaffected by my intrusion. He sat in perfect silence as I stood wide-eyed, motionless, and drawn in. I couldn't move. I was mesmerized.

Having just returned from church, this was a surprise lesson in the roots of religion. Ancient yogis perfected this state of Samadhi, and my dad was trying to do the same.

Between the book on the floor opened to the life story of Paramahansa Yogananda, and my father's vast knowledge of the secrets of the ages, my path forged before me. My mind conjured up images of faraway lands and epic battles over truth. I found a hundred reasons to be enthralled. Echoes of good vs. evil, right vs. wrong, and light vs. dark rang through my head even at that young age. My Polestar shone before me, right before my eyes and I followed it.

At that moment I pledged allegiance to something far greater than myself—a force beyond my understanding that

3

would always keep me heading in the right direction and striving for something higher. A path I anticipated with a five-year-old vigor that would age well through the years.

It was a path in search of God, and somehow I knew even then that I was in for a lifetime of intrigue. As my life unfolded, it became chapter after chapter of compelling drama, both good and bad, interpreted through the enlightened perception of my father and his teachers. When my father gave me his Samadhi inspired book, *Autobiography of a Yogi*, I could not put it down. All these years later, my vivid remembrance of him seated in lotus that Sunday morning long ago remains stamped in my memory.

And now today, on this bleak overcast day, mesmerized once again by that very same—very distinct—feeling, the circle came around.

*****

My father's and my mutual fascination with meditation began the moment I saw him seated in lotus. We started by simply placing a candle between us, staring into it, through it, and back into ourselves. We tried to silence our minds with repeated failure. What began as simple candle staring morphed into countless variations throughout the years, as our search for inner peace would take time and trial. Between the two of us, we discovered various practices. We tried everything, concentrating on God, concentrating on concepts such as love and peace, contemplating a series of positive thoughts, and focusing on our breath. As the years went by we dabbled in increasingly sophisticated forms of meditation.

This spiritual realm was my father's and my natural habitat. He would continually taunt me with mystical debuts, of which there were many. As soon as I could read he gave me the book, Garden of Eden, an enormous book which cataloged herbs, their healing properties, and resulting cures. I took it upon myself to master the art of prescribing herbal remedies and from then on dad steered ailing family members to the in-house "witch doctor" for a curing potion. Thankfully my remedies worked, and didn't require eight years and a white coat to cure a headache!

My father held a strong belief in the body's ability to heal itself given the right conditions. He believed that the body is a temple, a fantastic pharmacy, and the greatest doctor lives within. The inherent problem with this belief is learning to listen to our innate intelligence and to heed the voice of the inner doctor.

In my formative years, as my mother became a challenge to my sanity, my father became a reprieve for my soul. He became my compass, my navigator, my teacher and my role model.

He had a warm and quiet countenance about him that elicited positive comments from my friends and adults alike. It was a rare and noticeable quality.

Running the funeral business was his father's dying wish, and he was never in it for the money although it is how he made his living. His priority was to help people through the most difficult experience of their lives. Following a funeral service, families would come by to make their payment directly to the funeral home. My brother Mark was the one who received these payments, and he remembers a woman who made one $25 payment to her bill each year. It's all she could afford. Poor families did not have to pay, but they received the same decorum as well-to-do families.

My father dignified the deceased, rich or poor, and low-income families were so grateful that they could bury their loved ones with such respect. He graciously elevated their family, and no one knew they didn't pay a dime. His generosity and his compassionate nature are what gained him his reputation in the funeral business.

You would want to speak to my father if your loved one died. He embodied what it took to be a wonderful funeral director. He had "the gift."

He had an innate understanding of grief and the heartbreak of loss. He knew instinctively the important role that emotion plays in our life and the need to properly mourn. He helped people release their sorrow and transform their pain into something they could live with. He could return a smile to a grieving person's face which is the hardest thing to do in the funeral business. It's a gift, and my father had it.

This is what so many people reported to me. Story after story from people in town, his friends, even strangers, telling of his kindness, his compassion, his humility. He carried himself with a grace and authority that was gentle and highly regarded. People couldn't say enough about him. "There's only one Jacques" they would say. He was a class act. He was rare. And many people took the time to tell me so.

While my father conducted his funeral business with great dignity, his kids were obliviously playing behind the scenes.

In Junior high school, my best friend Sharon and I would often have to go to the funeral home to hitch a ride home from school from my dad. One day we came through the back entrance of the funeral home which leads directly into the garage. Sharon was sensitive and emotional and a little "jumpy" so she always felt a bit queasy coming into the funeral home.

The garage was large. It held two large black Chrysler Imperials used to transport immediate family members during the funeral procession. There was a hearse which transported the casket with the deceased from the church to the grave site. And a black Dodge station wagon used to pick up the body from the hospital and not draw attention.

To the right of the entrance were stairs that led to the main part of the funeral home and straight ahead was a cement ramp leading into the basement where the embalming took place. This basement also housed the staff break room, and this is where Sharon and I were headed to wait for my dad.

We walked down the ramp through the basement entrance, and our bodies shivered from the cold as we opened the door. The lights were dim in the hallway in contrast to the intense fluorescent lights coming from the embalming room on the right. A strong smell of formaldehyde, contained in embalming fluid, filled the entire basement. The floors were tile in the hallway, and shiny gray painted cement in the embalming room. Just past the embalming room, on the left side of the hallway, was an elevator. A little ways past the elevator was an office and then the break room.

The door was open to the embalming room, so we both paused when we got to it and snuck a peek inside. Sharon stood behind me, held onto my sides and peeked in. The sterile room had a stainless steel gurney on wheels next to a 50-gallon cylindrical tank with faucets attached to long rubber hoses. On a smaller stainless steel table on a crisp white terry cloth towel, was a scalpel, a knife, long thin scissors, forceps, metal hooks, a razor, cotton and two plastic eye caps. Looking at all of that made us both feel extra queasy, and I could feel Sharon's freezing hands through my shirt start to shake.

When you were our age, there was always this sinister, eerie feeling associated with death that made your skin crawl a little. And seeing this room didn't help. We quickly realized we didn't want to know what any of those things were for and we bolted.

Sharon was looking a little gray herself and started scurrying toward the break room when my dad called down to come upstairs. We were just passing the elevator, and so, for her sake, I pushed the button. She was stuck in place like glue, not moving a muscle. A few seconds later the elevator door started to open. But when it opened fully, smack in front of us on a gurney was a body lying beneath a white sheet.

Sharon shrieked and jumped back with her hand over her mouth, eyes like saucers. I convinced her that the body was dead and that we'd be upstairs in less than a minute. So she warily stepped with tiptoes onto the elevator, cramming herself against the elevator wall as far from the gurney as she could, hand still over her mouth. When the door closed behind us, I could see her trembling, poor thing. She was looking down, determined not to see the body on the gurney, her body stiff like the one on the table! She wasn't used to this as I was. As the elevator slowed down, I could see her body begin to relax, anticipating her escape. She started to look up.

But just as the door began to open, the body……..sat up! Her scream was so simultaneous with the movement of the body that I didn't know if her scream caused the body to sit up or if the body's sitting up caused her to scream! Then suddenly "the body" threw the sheet off, and it was…….my brother Mike!

Sharon flew out of the elevator and out the front door so fast that I didn't even see her exit. But I saw my horrified father run out the door after her. When I arrived at the door, I looked out to see him holding her while she trembled and cried. From a distance, I could hear him try to explain to her that boys will be boys but I don't know to this day whether she ever went back into the building. I'm sure she waited outside for any future rides home from my dad. I laid into Mike later that evening, but he thought it was the funniest thing in the world.

One colorful fall evening, my brother Marty and his friend Dave were kicked out of confirmation class by Grace Lutheran's head Pastor for wanting to discuss 'money is the root of all evil.' Dave mentioned that while the pastor was living on Skyline Drive, there were poor people's sons being killed in Vietnam. Marty agreed, and both were—as they called it—"freed" from the classroom. Two 13 year-olds on the loose! "

Marty walked Dave across Second Avenue and down the alley, to the back door of the funeral home. He tried turning the doorknob, but it was locked. He ran his fingers along the top edge of the door frame and found the spare key. As soon as he unlocked the door, he returned the key, walked in and locked the door behind them. Here is Dave's telling of the story:

"There I was in total darkness...locked in a funeral home ...probably with hundreds of dead people. It was dark.

"Len (his nickname for my brother) said, "Quiet David," and took me by the wrist. In total darkness, it seems like we may have gone up some stairs and turned a couple of corners. All I recall is...walking straight ahead for a long time...with Len guiding me by my wrist. There was only dead silence and darkness. I was impressed with Len's ability to see in the dark.

"He found a corner or a doorway or something, and we turned about 90 degrees and now walked slowly and cautiously...still in total darkness. Being that it was a colorful Fall day, being inside the funeral home made it blacker than ever.

"No one spoke a word...until...Len, softly said, "Stop. Put your arms straight down by your side, don't move them. Move left one foot, move forward three inches. Freeze. It's important you don't move at all. I'll be right back."

"Important I don't move? I got to thinking; did he just remember he needs to turn off the burglar alarm? Do funeral homes even have burglar alarms? My eyes strained to see. "My ears strained to hear. I think I may have started to imagine things. Was I hearing things? I strained my ears…it seemed like I heard a faint sound. It was the faintest of sounds...maybe. No, wait...there is a sound, isn't there? A faint sound. Is it music?

"The dark is changing color, isn't it? My ears and eyes were straining to detect a difference…or anything at all. Wait...yea...way off in the distance; there is the faint sound of organ music…isn't there? It's still dark but not as dark…is it? Was it organ music? Or was it all in my head?

"I couldn't tell...no wait, I can tell, it is organ music. Organ music like Dracula would play. It seems like it's getting less dark. Isn't it? What in the world?

"I closed my eyes and tried to relax my ears. Have I even been breathing? I took a deep breath and let it half out, slowly. I could feel my heart beat. I could hear my heart beat. I could feel my shirt bounce off my chest with each beat.   I'd never been in a funeral home before, much less left alone in the pitch dark and told not to move. Move! Where would I go? I can't see!

"There was a low distant, eerie sound of organ music, but it was getting closer. I opened my eyes; it was slowly, bit by bit, getting a little less dark…the music rose to a faint whisper. No doubt, it was eerie music!

"I'm not hallucinating; I'm not going crazy!

"The dark blackness continued to decrease, ever so slowly, my eyes strained to make out shapes. Without moving my limbs or body, I turned my head as far as it would go in both directions, just to try to see something, anything. Nothing. Wait, was that something? No, not enough light. I need more light to see.

"Slowly the music increased, and the light did too. I thought "I could now see shapes, but the shapes were lacking any familiar form. Now both the eerie organ music and light increased. I could see, I was standing right in front of something...a table...maybe...an altar? More light! I wanted more light. I needed more light to see.

 "My eyes struggled to focus as the volume of music increased. The light increased, too. It wasn't coming from a window; it was coming from…light fixtures. I looked up. What in the world? How can that be?

"I looked forward, the light increased. I looked down. Oh, MY GOD!!! My heart jumped, I'm standing right in front of a dead woman. Six inches from her coffin. I'm NOT hallucinating! She's in there, lying in there.

"She is silent, she is calm, she is not exactly smiling, but she looks very relaxed. She's NOT moving a bit. This is weird.

"Her hands are folded together on top of her stomach. Her gold wedding band is now shining in the light. Her fingernails are red and perfect. Her face is perfect. Her lipstick is as red as her nails. Her hair is permed. She is in a fancy dress. Her face so still. She only has one facial expression.

"DAMN IT!!! I jumped! Straight up…vertically, three feet…as I noticed Len standing right behind me …smiling. What a rush! It was straight out of a Vincent Price movie!

"All told, Len had been gone about four or five minutes. Seemed like hours.

"I could understand the music increasing in volume; that was easy to understand. However, it was the first time I'd ever experienced a dimmer switch.

"I'd never seen electric lights behave that way before.

"Still, she didn't move. She just preserved that same expression."

*****

This story reminds me of all the times my brothers and I would play hide-and-seek among the caskets in the showroom on the second floor. I was around six and tiny, so I could fit under the caskets easily, and no one could see me behind the skirts. One day I followed the lure of the baby blue satin pleating inside a dark mahogany casket with gold carrying handles and climbed on a stool to look inside. Just as I stood up fully balanced on the stool, my brother jumped out at me! I screamed and cried like my friend Sharon would years later. Inconsolably. I never told my dad about this casket experience because my brothers would have had my neck if I had. I knew where my loyalties had to be. There were three of them and just one of me.

My dad would have died himself had he known that my brother got inside one of the caskets! Dad ran a white-gloved affair. His staff had to run white gloves over the cars after washing them when preparing for a funeral. Little did he know he was striving for excellence and revering the deceased against all odds; and his four kids were his odds!

One time my cousin Hank and his friend Pete visited from Atlanta. They were older than we were—all of 17. They were hanging out one morning in what Hank called the "bowels" of the funeral home, the basement. My dad decided to satisfy their curiosity and invited them into the room to witness the embalming. I don't think either of them breathed during the whole process! I'm sure they decided right then and there that this was not what they wanted to do when they grew up!

My dad had many funerals going on during my cousin's visit, and he found that he had no one to drive a casket up to Minneapolis the following day. So he called on Hank and Pete to do it for him. Of course, they would do it! It was cool! But first, they had to drive their cargo to the drive-in hamburger stand to dazzle the girls. They thought it would be a great way to impress the carhop! Well, the guys may have thought they were cool, but the girls were grossed out!

The carhop zoomed up on her roller skates skillfully balancing their tray of food and drinks. She spotted the casket in the back, freaked out, tried to do a U-turn on her skates and sent the burgers and fries flying in every direction while she careened into the distance! What were those guys thinking?

Minneapolis had the closest crematorium to Eau Claire. After digging their burgers out of the dirt, Hank and Pete drove away with the tails between their legs and were back on task. They had named the deceased in their charge Ole. And Ole was in the back ready to go!

Arriving in Minneapolis, they drove down a narrow gravel road to the crematorium. They arrived at a monumental white cement building with double pillars. It looked stark and foreboding. The casket slid easily out the back of the Dodge and in through the main door. Minnesota state law required you to cremate the casket with the body. So when they got Ole inside, they followed him down to the basement and watched the crematorium workers place the whole casket into a large oven. They viewed the cremation through a small porthole.

The heat was set at 2200 degree F, and the boys watched, fascinated. It took awhile to burn through the brass casket. But then suddenly there was Ole, just lying there on this marble slab. The casket had vaporized. He was in a black suit. For a minute or so he just lay there, and then the heat started contracting his ligaments, and one of his arms moved! It was eerie for them to witness. Ole was reduced to dust except for his teeth. The crematorium worker swept up Ole and placed him into an urn and back they sped to Eau Claire.

Hank and Pete's telling of the story made me realize why death is so taboo in this country. It feels creepy and dark to most people. It is so far into the unknown that it scares us. We don't know how to act around it. We have no idea what death will be like. We can only imagine, and our imaginings take us to....well....the unimaginable!

The phones in our home were right outside my bedroom. Many times a week, in the middle of the night, my dad would get calls from the hospital to pick up bodies of patients who had just been pronounced dead. The decaying body of a loved one would be horrible for the family to see at the viewing. So he would get up anytime in the night to pick up the body to ensure it didn't decay before embalming. He wanted to make this traumatizing experience as pleasant and smooth as possible for their families.

My brother Mark worked at the funeral home in many capacities. One afternoon he was the hearse driver for a prominent Eau Claire family. Hundreds of people were at this particular service. After the service was over the pall bearers carried the casket to the hearse. After they had rolled it up on the platform and into the hearse, Mark's job was to secure the platform, so it didn't roll out during the drive.

The pall bearers cars and the family cars were right behind the hearse that Mark was driving. When they were about halfway to the cemetery, they started up a steep hill. But halfway up the hill, Mark heard a grumbling sound coming from the back of the hearse. He turned around to see the platform and casket rolling toward the back door. His life at this job passed before him as he imagined the casket landing on the family's car behind him! He swung his right arm around and with herculean effort was barely able to grab the handle on the casket and to hang onto it for dear life while continuing to drive up the steepest part of the hill. Imagine—his left hand on the steering wheel, his right hand hanging onto that heavy casket up the hill all the way to the cemetery. Thank God he was blessed with long arms and quick reflexes!

Floral arrangements were left at the funeral home after each service. The families would have the flowers delivered to specific people, and the funeral home would keep the rest. It was Mark's job to deliver the flowers, and he roped in his best friend Bill to help him make the deliveries. Leftover arrangements would often go to a little old lady who lived down the street. She made homemade apple wine, and they were always offered a glass when they brought her flowers. One day the light bulb went off! If a little old lady would give them wine in exchange for flowers, maybe they could attract some beautiful girls with these bouquets.

It was a typical summer evening, and everyone met at Eau Claire's "four corners." Mark and Bill decided to cruise through town in the black Dodge. They spotted one of Mark's old flames, Weedie, hanging out with two of her friends Judy and Kitty, so they stopped to visit. They asked the girls if they wanted to go to the Pronto Pup, a local drive-in restaurant, and the girls hopped in.

Several days later a large bouquet of flowers was delivered to Judy's house.

Judy's mother gave the flowers to her, but there was no card attached. Judy thought, "These flowers look like they came from a funeral!" and asked if they were delivered in a black car. Her mom confirmed that they had. Judy called Kitty, and Kitty had also received a large bouquet with a missing card, and hers had also been delivered in a black car. That night on the four corners, the girls spotted the black Dodge and yelled out, "Hey boys! You been delivering flowers lately?" Well, nothing blossomed for Bill, but it was a life changer for Mark! Judy married him, and they've lived happily ever after!

After the body is embalmed, a cosmetologist restores the face to its lifelike appearance. Then the hair is shampooed and styled like in a salon. Our mother was trained to do this job. When the body is ready for viewing, it is carefully placed in the casket and moved to the visitation room.

One day, I was probably seven, while waiting for my dad to take me home, I snuck into the visitation room when no one was there. As I curiously crept closer to the casket, I noticed something disturbing. I peeked over the edge of the casket to confirm my suspicions and saw to my horror that my favorite bow was in the dead woman's hair! I couldn't believe it. MY bow! I stood as tall as I could on my tiptoes to try to grab it, but my small arms couldn't reach it.

I ran downstairs, got a stool and ran it over to the casket as fast as I could before anyone caught me. I wanted my bow back! I got up on the stool and then froze. I looked down at her, and I was scared. After the experience with my brother jumping out of the casket, I wasn't so sure that this woman wouldn't do the same if I tried to reclaim my bow! So I stopped. I stared at it in her hair for a while trying to will if off but to no avail. So far no one had caught me in the forbidden room, so I jumped down from the stool and ran it back to the basement. I sat in the break room and waited for my dad.

That night when I got home, I threw a little fit about my bow. My mother's defense was that this woman looked too plain, so my mother needed to "gussy her up." But I cried so hard, and she felt so badly that she went out and bought me new bows in every color she could find. My mother was stylish, and she always wanted to make people prettier than they were. So my bow was sacrificed for the cause. I got over it.

*****

There are as many funeral home stories as people who have died. But as people died and death touched my young life, it was always my father to whom I would turn for comfort.

When President John F. Kennedy was assassinated, we were all sent home from school. I remember sitting on my bed, crying my eyes out when my dad walked in and sat down next to me. He spoke softly, calmly and with certainty. He had an aura about him that I would bask in at times like this. He was serious but not sad really, and something in the way he spoke opened my heart to understand his message. He explained, "President Kennedy had an easy passing. He crossed over to the other side with clear consciousness. He was not confused, and he made an easy transition to the other side. He is doing just fine."

I was accustomed to talking with my father like this. I found myself slowly calming down as I listened to him speak. The details he was sharing with me provided such great relief. So I accepted the passing of President Kennedy with a much lighter heart and a greater understanding of "passing" and "crossing over." It is only today that I wonder how in the world he knew the details that he shared! How did he know that Kennedy had crossed over to the other side without any confusion? How did he know he was doing "just fine"? How did he know any of this?

As it turns out, he knew many interesting things.

I asked him why people say, "Rest in Peace" and he explained the soul needs a rest from a lifetime of exertion. I had no idea a soul would need to rest. I asked him why, since the body was dead, and he explained it is the soul that does all the work. I pondered that idea. I thought the soul simply "was," but found out the soul has a big job to do.

As the years passed, I came to my own understanding of this.

In real estate, there is a term "as platted" as opposed to "as built." It was designed to be one way (as platted) but turned out a different way (as built). In one of my real estate transactions, when they built the road, they built it far from the granted right-of-way. It would have cost a fortune to change the road to match the platted right-of-way, so the easy fix was to change the deed to read "as built." So we did that to make the road legal.

In our life, it may not be so different. We come in with a plat map. It's where we're supposed to go and how we're supposed to be. The soul comes in with a certain plan, things to do, goals to reach, gifts to give, things to work out, and karma to finish. However, because of our decisions along the way, we may veer off the platted course. Our life becomes "as built." It becomes what we make of it. But there was a "plat" in place when we got here. As we begin our journey and make our choices, some of those choices cause us to veer from the original design. The farther we veer, the harder we have to work to return to the original plat.

After making zillions of choices in our life, we may be in a very different place then we were meant to be. So the soul has the job of getting us back on track and aligning our life with our original plan so we can live our life "as platted." Our free will can take us off course or keep us on track, and it usually does a little of both. We know when we are on track, we can feel it. We also know when we're not.

When I think about it this way, I realize the soul needs to rest. I understand the job it has to do and how hard it has to work to get into alignment. If we could superimpose our individual map (as built) over the original map (as platted), we could see how far we have to go. We could make choices to maneuver the road to match the original plat. We have to pay the price, but it is worth any price to bring them back into alignment.

That, I believe, is why we are here, to accomplish what we came for, to give our gifts, work out the issues, finish our karma, live our full potential. The soul has a big job. I now understand "rest in peace." But only now. So many years later.

One night after dinner, I was sitting at the kitchen counter on a stool doing my eighth-grade homework. Dad was in the kitchen not too far from me. After several minutes I realized I hadn't heard a peep from him, no sound, no movement, nothing. So I looked up and curiously found him staring into the freezer. From my vantage point, sitting at the counter, I didn't see much happening. Only my dad staring into the freezer.

I waited for something to happen, and finally, it begged the question," Dad, what are you doing?" "I'm trying to manifest ice cream," he said without breaking his stare. A split second passed, and we both burst out laughing. But I can still see the impish expression on his face as he said that.

That lead to the first of many lectures about the gray matter in the brain not knowing the difference between imagination and reality. This must have been something he learned from personal success guru Napoleon Hill. "Think, and you shall have it" became my mantra for manifestation! He had me constantly imagining what it was that I wanted—clearly and concisely down to the last detail.

Mary Quant mini dress, red velvet with lace collar and matching cuffs, size 3, P. 13 in the September issue of the Fashion Catalog. I imagined it in that amount of detail…and in my mind I already owned it. I was told if I did that it would be mine. I must say that HIS MONEY ended up getting me that red dress! I thanked him profusely for teaching me how to get what I wanted. He couldn't argue with me. Either way, I manifested it!

Oddly enough, what I wanted most was that experience of silence we were looking for in our many years of trying different meditations.

Not only did my dad show me the power of the mind and the intelligence of the body, but he also taught me about the nature of others and the power of their intentions. We live in a world where religion is paramount, and fanatics kill to advance their belief. My father took me out onto our deck as a child and had me look through the barrel of a large white telescope. He pointed out the vast array of stars and planets and explained how the universe holds all the answers. He explained that what we see "out there" is also within ourselves. He extolled the power within.

I only understood that many years later when I learned Transcendental Meditation (TM) and experienced "the within" for myself. While on a TM weekend residence course, I saw the film, "Powers of 10". It depicted the relative scale of the universe in factors of 10. It began with a man on the beach, and the camera zoomed out by powers of 10 (i.e. 10 times more magnification every 10 seconds). It showed the entire universe in periods of rest and activity as the lens zoomed out.

Then the lens zoomed back to the man on the beach. This time it zoomed in by powers of 10. Shockingly, there was the exact same pattern of rest and activity when zooming in. This time, however, instead of planets they were cells in the body. They looked the same and followed the exact patterns of the moving universe. The film ended inside a proton of a carbon atom within the DNA molecule in a white blood cell. And that looked exactly like the farthest reaches of the known universe!

That is when the light bulb switched on for me, and I remembered back to that moment on our deck.

Somewhere between the mystics and the scientists is an intelligent force where every part has its purpose. The cosmos is extraordinarily harmonious and perfect. It was there, on our deck, that I learned that Christian Saints and Indian Yogis have the same goal. That all religions are different, but all strive for the same purpose. Union with God. Understanding of Love. Discovery of Truth. The search for—real truth—is universal.

Truth is so diverse in its interpretation and equally diverse in its search. Some seek truth from others; some believe ancient texts, some believe in Mother Earth, some seek truth within, some don't believe in anything, some believe in everything—all according to their particular window of perception and all true for them. I realized, for thousands of years, people have killed to defend, prove or protect their truth. The search is so powerful that people around the world passionately uphold that which they feel is right. I understood the fuel behind some of the world's greatest tragedies.

Through my father, I developed a huge perspective on life and wide recognition and acceptance of different beliefs. I realized then and understand now that everyone has their own soul leading them through the exact experiences they need to get where they are going. Everyone has their own truth guiding them, their own Polestar, so to speak, and it is real, right, and true for them. I have no right to judge another soul's path and believe that no one else has the right to judge mine either.

I heard the teacher of TM, Maharishi Mahesh Yogi, say that karma is unfathomable. The workings of karma are way beyond our human ability to grasp. Therefore we cannot judge anyone for anything. No one can back up far enough to see the whole impressive picture that created an event, to see why things had to happen the way they did. No one can see the entire karmic workings that would make sense out of everything and explain the actions of another.

I cannot put myself in anyone else's shoes. None of us can. It is their experience and try as we might, we cannot have their exact experience because we are not in their body in their exact circumstances. We cannot fathom another's reality because we are not them. It's with this belief that I think we, as a people, could benefit from a commitment to non-judgment.

After I had started college, following my father's 'your body is a temple' mantra, I evolved into following a vegetarian lifestyle. Most young adults go through different phases, and an herbivore's lifestyle fit well with me. When I returned home, it didn't take much persuasion for my father to join in and to take the concept one step further by becoming....a liquid vegetarian! He felt the idea of assimilating vitamins and minerals more directly into the system caused less physical stress and was far superior to eating, chewing and digesting.

Around this time I gave him the book, *The Findhorn Garden*, for Father's Day. According to the people at Findhorn in Scotland, in their own description, elemental beings, or nature spirits called "Devas," live inside each plant and telepathically relay to the gardeners what is needed for the plant to grow. Interestingly, the communications were also a metaphor for living our human life. Here is an example of one communication that has remained in my memory since I read the book many years ago:

Tend My special flowers with very special care. Flowers

unfold slowly and gently, bit by bit in the sunshine, and a soul, too, must never be pushed or driven but unfolds in its own perfect timing to reveal its true wonder and beauty.
The Findhorn Garden, P. 50

Another quote from the book:

Indeed, the growth of the garden is symbolic of the growth of the soul. The proper environment must be created, weeds that might choke out the finer, more delicate qualities of the soul must be removed, and all actions must be guided by the love that fulfills all laws. P. 30

Through communication with these elemental beings and close cooperation with nature, the Findhorn people learned how to properly grow their gardens. Their vegetables grew to gigantic proportions, and Findhorn Garden became famous for its magnificent gardens. Since 1962, legendary plants, herbs and vegetables have been growing out of barren, sandy soil, making Findhorn Garden a stunning and thriving horticultural masterpiece.

Well, my father read the book and…lo and behold! He grew a garden out of sand in his back yard! He lived in Pueblo West, Colorado so there was little fertile soil, only sand. It goes without saying that this became a popular topic in his then small town where there wasn't another patch of green in sight. When, dumbfoundedly, the neighbors asked how he achieved his mysterious sand garden, he casually replied, "I speak to the Devas." As one might imagine, the neighbors no longer asked! Today I wonder what in the world they must have thought he was talking about when he referenced his conversations with those creative plant spirits!

One Father's day I gave my dad a book about Shamans assuming he'd be interested in my newly found fascination.

His response to my gift was that he had tried to become a Shaman 30 years prior. Really? You tried to BECOME a Shaman? What did you do? Call Africa?

One day, I complained to my father that I wasn't ever hungry. He said, "Then don't eat." What a piece of advice coming from my father that I shouldn't eat! I asked," What should I do?" He answered, "Wait until you're hungry and then eat." So I waited until I was hungry and 14 days later ate some food. It's amazing how I felt!

My mind and body could function with a level of extraordinary clarity that I had never experienced before.

I repeated his instructions many times after that and only ate when I was hungry. Sometimes I went for 10 days, sometimes for only two, sometimes for a much longer period. It was easy and felt natural to me. Dad told me I must be partially "breatharian."

Breatharians have the ability to take in nutrients from prana, or life force, produced by the sun. It's a different sort of nutrition. I don't think many people are geared for that, but I seemed to be able to go for long periods of time without eating food. I wouldn't plan for these fasts; I just wouldn't eat until I was hungry. Sometimes that was many weeks later. Sometimes it was the next day. I drank when I was thirsty, and it was not a big deal. I just followed what my body wanted. You can imagine, I was a popular date! Didn't cost him a dime!

Dad explained to me that too much undigested food clogs our digestive system. It doesn't allow our cells to function properly, resulting in our minds not thinking clearly and our bodies not feeling as energetic as they could. He explained how the mind and body could function far beyond most people's comprehension if only allowed the opportunity. It is important that the body is healthy and strong so that the soul can shine through it.

The soul's expression through the body and mind is what is important, not the body or mind per se. We are not our body, we are not our mind, but we are our soul. We take care of the body and the mind best by leaving it in a simpler state so the soul can shine through and align with its purpose. "That's how it is," he would tell me. (i.e., the "plat map.")

Oh! So much that my father and I shared! We fasted, we juiced, we ate raw, we drank spirulina shakes. Vegetarian. Liquid vegetarian! We wore black plastic sunglasses with little holes in them to exercise our eyes. We sun bathed our eyes for better vision and sun gazed in the early morning to fill our cells with full spectrum light. This was all before I reached 20! And this was before all of these things were commonly known.

*****

In my third year of college, our literature class was studying Procol Harum's "Lighter Shade of Pale" (You have to love college!) A fellow student who always sat next to me, one day leaned over to me and asked," Do you want to get higher than drugs and stay there?' I thought it was a trick question! "Ahhh….yeeaaaah!" So he told me about this particular meditation that was taking the campus by storm. That night I went to the introductory lecture and was instructed into this technique of meditation the following Saturday and...

BINGO! There it was! Clear as a bell—that quiet mind I sought for so long.

It was one of those experiences you never forget. Pure silence. Pure unbounded consciousness. A still mind. The

clouds parted, and the sun came shining through. So easily.
So naturally. It was the fulfillment of that Sunday-after-
church experience that my dad was trying to achieve. Jesus
said the kingdom of heaven is within and heaven's doors
flung wide open that day! I experienced heaven within.

My heart fell to its knees in gratitude.

I now knew how my father and I would reach Samadhi. I
had experienced it firsthand. That day we flipped the page
to find the missing chapter in the novel of our lives. 'Part
II' was about to begin.

After years of trying other methods, we found silence. It
was a miracle. Transcendentalists have tried to describe it,
and even the most glorious descriptions cannot adequately
capture the essence of this experience. There are no words.
Absolute silence. Complete tranquility. Just you, fully
awake within yourself, with no distraction and no other
intruding thought. Every human being yearns for this,
every religion speaks of it, and for us, it was delivered in
spades. Our gray matter manifested it! At last.

TM was notably different from the other meditations we
had tried. It wasn't a meditation we could learn from a
book. In other practices, we were either concentrating or
contemplating. Both kept our mind on the surface. There
was such a clear difference in this meditation. This
technique allowed our mind to go deep within—quickly—
and to experience total silence.

I found the benefits staggering. I was only looking to quiet
my mind, but the side effect of doing so was that I felt
much more energy and my mind was clearer. I became
organized in my work. I slept better than I had ever slept in
my life and I finished my last year of college with straight
A's. My brain was clear, and I understood the information I

was studying…and remembered it because I understood it. My mind was experiencing deeper levels of the thinking process which allowed deeper levels of understanding.

Prior to this, I only washed my laundry when it piled so high it fell off the chair. Now I washed it and put it away, and it never piled up again. Fits of tossing and turning at night ended. My cupboards became organized, my desk got all tidied up, and I was on a roll!

Nothing else produced this effect. Not even close. Concentration held my attention on the surface of my mind thinking about a single object. Contemplation held my attention on a series of thoughts. All thinking. All on the surface of the mind. During TM the mind is naturally attracted to increasingly quieter levels of thinking. It becomes so quiet it transcends thinking altogether. It experiences the source of thought which is silence. And silence is by far the most charming experience to an active mind.

The benefits of transcending have been widely researched.

Scientists discovered that both mind and body are affected simultaneously during the practice of TM. As the mind settles down, the brain waves go from a chaotic state to an increasingly coherent state. This happens within each hemisphere of the brain as well as between the two hemispheres. When the mind experiences silence, the brain waves are coherent.

Correspondingly, as the body settles down, oxygen consumption decreases, galvanic skin response changes, and the body experiences a deep rest which is much deeper than the deepest point of sleep; therefore, it releases deeper rooted stresses than even deep sleep can release.

No wonder I felt so good! I had less stress, more energy,

and a clear, organized mind.

This simple technique changed my life…by fulfilling it. It allowed me to experience pure consciousness within on a daily basis, which I did twice a day from that time on.

I think we all have that same feeling—deep inside—that there is more. More to life than what we are living and more to us than who we are right now. I have always been looking for the "real me," the whole me, me that is everything I know I can be. Mother Nature delivered myself to me that day in that profound experience of silence.

Although an ancient technique, Maharishi taught it in such a way to make it easy for westerners to learn. I wanted to teach others what I had learned, so I became a teacher of TM, and my father was my first student. I was able to reciprocate to him in kind for what he had given me growing up. He paved the way for the next phase of my life where I started to give back what I had learned.

I spent the next 20 years teaching TM around the world. Speaking with my dad spawned many interesting conversations about the simultaneity of events in time and space, free will, and past lives. He said we merely perceive that we live one life at a time.

He said you could pick any moment of time and focus on it and get the whole picture of that "time" or lifetime. It hit me like "pick a card, any card." Something I struggled to understand then, but liken it today to the Internet. Let's say the Internet is your whole soul's journey through life, in every incarnation, in all of creation, in all of time. If you click on it, you'd have the whole picture of one lifetime. It is only one piece of the entire puzzle. But like the puzzle, it all exists simultaneously. It's like one giant mosaic.

I think that concept is extremely difficult for the human mind to grasp. He seemed to have a handle on it. The Internet and the puzzle are the only analogies that help me understand it. That's why only using a small portion of our potential is frustrating to me…and why I consciously choose to expand it every day.

Dad told me if we could travel forward in time and look at a situation we wished had turned out differently, we would be surprised to find out that it didn't matter much. We end up where we are supposed to. Therefore, he told me to "have no regrets." We are all doing our best, no matter how it looks to ourselves or others.

All of this naturally led me to the question of free will. What I gathered from our many conversations was that we do have free will, but we also have a bigger destiny. Recently a great teacher, Bill Bauman, succinctly clarified it for me. He said, "Frequently humans are allowed not only the use of free will but the privilege of using that free will to alter or change our human conditions. However, when a specific condition or outcome is "destined"—that is, when it's so divinely inspired that every aspect of nature is dredged up to make it happen, no matter what—no amount of free will can or will change that destiny. Thus, in conclusion, "Free Will will always bow to Destiny!"

So it seems no matter what path we take, all roads lead to Rome. We will get there because we are always doing the best we can do. Everyone is, regardless of how circuitous their lives may appear. Even when we don't think we are doing well or we think we could have done better, we are following our specific course according to our level of awareness and our unfathomable karma. If we could have done better, we would have.

My father often talked about how we create our reality. Our

outer circumstances reflect our inner life. Everything outside of us is a replica of everything within us. Including that which is WAY outside us—in the universe. "As the microcosm so the macrocosm." Everything affects everything in the universe, so I should watch my thoughts and intentions and the words that I speak.

Growing up with my father wasn't so much about playing girls softball and talking about boyfriends as it was conversations about these topics. All of his wisdom was fascinating to me from such a young age and became even more so when I got old enough to understand what he was saying. There are many times that I wish I could bring him back to pick his brain.

Above all, he taught me to trust my own experience, beyond all dogma, doctrines, philosophy, books, opinions, and ideology; beyond anything outside of myself. He encouraged me to trust my own truth and walk my own path.

*****

Fast forward 20 years.

It was a gorgeous 4th of July in 1995 in Fairfield Iowa. The sun was bright against the blue sky, not too hot, just a beautiful day after the rain cleared any dust from the air. I was driving. My father was in the front seat of my car, and my friend Amshiva was in the back. She sat forward in her seat so she could hear the story my father was telling of Paramahansa Yogananda's death. I remember the story because my father had given me Yogananda's book, "Autobiography of a Yogi" soon after I found him meditating in his boxers that Sunday long ago. It was the first spiritually oriented book I had ever read. It was a

31

fascinating book because it describes events that are vastly different from anything we experience in our everyday life.

My dad explained that on the last day of his life, Yogananda was on stage and had spoken to a large group of people. When he finished his talk, he walked to the back of the stage, sat down in full lotus and silently drifted into mahasamadhi. Mahasamadhi is the final transcendence or death. According to Wikipedia, mahasamadhi is the act of consciously and intentionally leaving one's body at the time of enlightenment. A realized yogi (male) or yogini (female) who has attained the state of <u>samadhi</u> (enlightenment), will, at an appropriate time, consciously exit from their body. This is known as mahasamadhi.

When he finished telling the story, my father said matter-of-factly to Amshiva and me that he was going to do the same. He was going to choose his moment of death and then exit. Goose bumps rippled across my skin! Amshiva and I shot a quick glance at each other, both knowing that this is exactly what he would do. It took a minute to get my mouth closed after my jaw dropped. I am telling you, truth has a way of letting you know it's true.

I remembered my father telling me a long time before this, that life comes and goes with the breath. We come into this world on our first inhalation, and we leave on our last exhalation. From the minute we take our first breath, we are taking in prana, or life force. We take it in constantly throughout our life. At exactly six months before we are to die we start breathing out prana, and letting our life force go. If we could know that exact moment of transition between taking in prana and letting prana go out, we would know the exact moment of our death.

How about that for a father! He shared such thought-provoking and profound tidbits with me.

My boyfriend once said to me, "Beware of geeks bearing gifts!" as he tossed me a bag of cotton balls, dental floss, and toothpaste. It, oddly, made me think of saints bearing gifts. Not only beware of them but be ready for them. Make yourself ready for the best gifts of your life—and much better gifts than dental floss! Little did I know that in 1996, exactly six months—to the day—since my father told me he was going to choose his moment of death, he did. He left this life, and I was in for the signature gift of my lifetime.

I never feared my father's death. I lived my life knowing that his soul would somehow make sure I was there when he passed. We had such a deep spiritual connection throughout our life that I knew I'd be with him at his most hallowed moment of all.

On a cold winter afternoon in 1996, I walked into my apartment with two of my friends, and the phone was ringing. I ran to answer it and caught it just before the last ring. I was out of breath when I blurted out my rushed hello. The call was from some unknown doctor in some unknown hospital in a town I had never heard of near Kansas City. I listened…and listened…he seemed to be saying something but…the words escaped me and became more and more imperceptible. I got as far as…"I'm sorry"…and I let the phone fall from my hands.

The blood drained from my head so quickly that I reached for a chair and slumped into it, blank. I remained in this state so long that my friends had to handle things for me. The only thing I was certain of was that my heart was still beating. My empty stare was joggled when we couldn't reach my brother Marty. His phone was out of order, and we couldn't reach him to tell him our father had died. So we concocted a plan to send a pizza to his house with a note for him to call me. That was weird. He was like, "Ummmm I got this pizza from you…..and…why

33

exactly?" I didn't think to call the sheriff's office and have them give my brother the message.

After all the details were worked out, John and Amshiva and I ceremoniously lit a candle for my father, said silent prayers, and sat for a long time, praying, crying, feeling. I could feel my father's presence in the room with us, so I spoke softly to him. "Dad, I've always come to you when someone has died, and now I am coming to you for you. I told him that, of all people in my life, there should be nothing left unresolved between us. I learned the lesson of resolve from my mother when she died, and I have kept all my relationships resolved since then. So there should be nothing left unresolved with the most important relationship in my life, my father.

However, I had two things to resolve with him. I asked him to help me in any way he could, by speaking through other people, speaking directly to me, showing me signs, or whatever he needed to do to get through to me. The first situation to bring to resolution was simply that I didn't get to see him again. My friend John and I were about to have Sunday brunch with him at Everybody's in Fairfield in a couple of days, but we never got the chance to do that. I never got to see him again.

The second thing to resolve was that I didn't get to spend as much time with him while he was in Fairfield as I normally would have. My boyfriend, at that time, was obsessed and controlling. Every time I would have naturally gone to see my dad, to watch a football game or play golf or whatever, my boyfriend would object. So I had to deal with that rather than be with my dad.

Later that night, when we were finished with all the details, I sat down on the edge of my bed, overwhelmed with grief, exhausted, still in shock, and closed my eyes. I was feeling the deep sorrow of not being able to see my father ever again. In my mind's eye, I imagined us at our Sunday brunch at Everybody's. I was seeing him bent over his tray of mashed potatoes as he carried the tray back to our table.

Just then.....something extraordinary happened. He gave me a vision of his spirit exiting from his body. I saw him lying down, and I saw his spirit leave through the top of his head and suddenly appear before me as this huge, I mean HUGE, way-up-in-the-sky HUGE Being of light. It seemed to be on the level of an Ascended Master type of Being—huge! It took me by surprise, and I laughed out loud. It was so his sense of humor to say to me,
"Hmmmmmm....mashed potatoes or this, mashed potatoes or this. Honey, I just didn't need to come back for those mashed potatoes!" He had chosen his most exalted moment to exit from his body…just like he said he would do six months earlier while driving in the car with Amshiva and me.

My dad died on January 4, 1996. The conversation in the car about his choosing his moment of death had taken place on July 4, 1995, exactly six months earlier.

This experience was so powerful it immediately resolved the fact that I didn't get to see him again. His exit was perfect and utterly brilliant! Absolutely in divine order.

The first thing needing resolution was resolved in his vision to me. The second resolution was about to come.

My father's right-hand man bought the funeral business from him when my dad retired. Upon hearing of my father's death, Jerry warned me not to view his body. Since he was not going to be embalmed, decay would begin immediately, and he was certain that my father would not

35

want me to see his body in that condition.

But I really wanted to see him. I needed to see his face.

After seeing my mother's face when she died and seeing the pain in her expression, I wanted to see my father's face. I learned from my mother that you could see a person's life and death in their face at death. Everyone remarked on how beautiful my mother looked and how peaceful she looked as she lay in her casket, but I didn't see it that way. She was beautiful in her royal blue blouse and her striking whitish-blonde hair, but behind what others perceived as a smile, I saw anguish.

It was shocking to me and unforgettable to see the true face of death. To see behind the peaceful look. Anticipating a very different look than my mother's, I wanted to see my father.

There were treacherous ice storms around Kansas City. For five days my father's body lay anonymously in a hospital morgue, and I could not get there. At 20 degrees and ice still falling, it was worth heeding the undertaker's advice not to come. Having been an undertaker's daughter myself, I respected his wish not to have me end up like my father!

When the ice storms finally subsided, we piled into the car. By the time we got there, I did not want to see him anymore. I knew what condition he would be in and I knew that now I should heed Jerry's advice. Nonetheless, when I arrived, I called the funeral home, and the funeral director insisted I view the body because it had not been identified. On hearing this, I began to feel queasy. I had been warned not to view him on the day after his death. Now it was six days later, and I could hardly sleep knowing what I would face the next morning.

I was feeling decidedly more squeamish as we set out for

the funeral home. I mentally steadied myself to witness my father in an advanced state of decay.

When we got out of the car, I clutched my coat in the front of me and hunched forward for extra protection against the wind, but it couldn't protect me from the bitter chill in my psyche. John and I walked up the gradual incline of the sidewalk toward the red brick building with white marble columns that stood regally at the top of the hill, like a monument. The closer I got to the building, the more I was haunted by his warnings not to be here. Nevertheless, I reached for the long bronze handle and walked inside.

We were struck by rich burgundy textures, gold ornamentation, several pictures of Jesus and immense silence.

We were greeted by a soft-spoken gentleman in a dark suit. After taking our coats, he led us down a dark hallway to the rear of the building.

As we walked in silence, my heart was pounding over the loud tick of the antique clock. I noticed the floral aroma fade to something quite dank and musty. The kind man stopped and opened a door which sent a sudden waft of cool air our way. Then he stepped aside to allow us to enter first. An even colder chill ran through me as my eyes adjusted to the dim light of the room. Suddenly I was gripped by an emotion I was not prepared for. I stood frozen in place. I was absolutely mesmerized by what I saw. At the end of the room…..this very long room was…..my father.

I just stood there. Staring.

Nothing in the room was moving except the rise and fall of my chest. Not a sound except the beat of my heart. Nothing in my life had prepared me for this moment.

I could see his body lying on a gurney across the room. I was intensely transfixed. As I slowly began the long walk toward the gurney, it seemed the room was filled with some subtle golden light. It was very surreal, like something not of this earth. I was spellbound. I had experienced this very distinct feeling before.

The funeral director placed a chair next to the gurney so I could step up and see his face. It felt as though I levitated up onto the chair in one smooth move. From a place of deep trepidation, something altogether dreamlike emerged, and I could not believe what I was looking at. Looking down at his face, I saw the most beautiful sight I have ever seen in my life.

Not only was there no decay, but I was looking at the most beatific face I have ever seen, and a smile like none I have seen on this earth. It was otherworldly. Around his face and about 12 inches out, was this absolutely perceptible light. It was a very distinct, palpable, clear, white, see-through light visible to the eye. I reached toward his face and put my fingers inside the light, rubbing my thumb across my fingers to try to feel it. It felt just like air, but it was distinctly different from the air around it. It was the light you see around the heads of saints and holy people.

Ecstasy filled every cell in my body. I was rapt. I tingled. I was filled with bliss and was overcome with God's presence. The divine radiance that filled my father also filled me.

I saw the light of God in that face. And the justness of all life. Everything in life is divine and holy, but this was holiness I had only seen in pictures.

I saw his whole life add up to this moment of death. I saw his exit right out the top of his head that he had shown me in the vision while sitting on my bed the night he died. I saw his entire life add up to this moment that I was seeing in his face. Tears ran down my face as I cried, "YES! YES! YES!"

I can only imagine what the funeral director was thinking. In fact, he muttered quietly, "It is a beautiful smile isn't it?" From his perspective, it was a beautiful smile, but from mine, it was utterly rapturous. I saw all his incredible kindness add up to <u>this moment</u>. His unquestionable love amid great adversity add up to <u>this moment.</u> I saw every choice he made throughout his life add up to <u>this moment</u>.

It was a powerful sight to witness. It was the power of God. His exit from this planet was extraordinary. I'm telling you it was glorious. The most glorious exit from his body and from this earthly life that I could ever imagine. He was in an exalted state of holiness. Mahasamadhi. Divine essence was emanating from him. Not only had his body NOT decayed in these six days, but there was tangible light effusing from his body. He had the most beatific, beyond-this-earth smile, his eyes were aimed upward toward the top of his head, and he gave me the greatest spiritual wisdom of my life. He was in a state of grace, and so was I.

<u>This moment</u> of his death revealed to me the purpose of life on earth.

What I got by looking into his face in death was:

> *At every given moment we have the choice to love open-heartedly or not, and when we get to the end of our life, it's all going to add up to the choices we made at every given moment.*

This was his farewell gift to me.

My father chose to keep his heart open in the face of

adversity and struggle. He never closed his heart down. Instead, he opened and embraced every single raw and painful event and went straight through the middle of it. No denial, no closing down. I watched it. I was in awe. Every time. Love prevailed. Every time. No matter what and no matter how difficult or grave the pain.

I believe there is an energy generated when someone leaves this earth that is there especially for those close to them. If your awareness is receptive to it, there are beautiful spiritual gifts given which allow you a greater awareness of the divine in your life.

Remembering their life and sensing their nature helps us to learn from them. We integrate them into our heart, and they live within us, so they are not forgotten. This serves to bless both the grieving and the departed.

When I saw my father's choices throughout his life add up to this exalted last moment, it ignited something in me. I became acutely aware that every moment in our life offers us a choice. And we can choose to keep our heart open in love or not.

The drama of life, by its very nature, offers challenges and choices at every turn. We live in a fluctuating state of change. We are constantly faced with choices, and every choice is significant. Every choice we make has consequences, and our life becomes the cumulative result of our choices. If we choose to become a doctor rather than a movie producer; if we choose to go to Florida State University rather than Oxford; if we choose to cut someone out of our life rather than forgive them; if we choose to invest in a high-risk investment rather than a conservative one; if we choose to marry our high school sweetheart even though we know it is wrong. The choices in our life are endless and the consequences equally as endless. Every choice we make is absolutely significant.

But the choice I am referring to is a different kind of choice. The choice to love no matter what other choices you have made and no matter what circumstances your choices have put you in. It's a choice of how to act and be in each moment. I saw, looking at the face of my father, just how significant this kind of choice is. In those moments of choice, we find our true self.

We have a choice how we live every one of our moments on this physical plane. We can open our hearts in love every time we have a choice to….or not. We can love even though someone has wronged us….or not. We can keep our heart open in love in the face of humiliation and despair….or not. We can get angry and close down….or not. We can choose to be kind, or we can choose to be mean-spirited. We can let more love in, or we can shut our heart down. We have that choice. And this is the most significant choice we ever make. And we constantly make it. It is our biggest challenge because it is hard to do. This is the choice I am talking about.

The choice to keep our hearts open in love through all things….no matter how hard.

In the end, love is all that matters. In the end, that's all there is. The choice to love is the only thing that is important. This is the wisdom that was left to me as a blessing from my father. To keep our hearts open in love at every given moment. And that…in the end…everything turns out exactly as it should according to our choices.

After viewing the body, I told John this is not a body I wanted to burn. This is a body I wanted to place under glass because anyone seeing his face in death would know the purpose of life on earth. To love open-heartedly at all times, through all things. I wanted my brothers to see his face. I wanted my ex-husband to see his face.

I wondered how long his body would remain in a state of non-decay. According to his autobiography, Yogananda's body still had not decayed after 20 days. It remained suspended in an elevated state of grace.

After escorting my father's body to the crematorium, the crematorium attendant said to us, "Can you believe this guy? He's been dead for six days! He hasn't even decayed." With that, he shoved his body feet first into the furnace with his "World's Greatest Grandpa" sweatshirt on, the long-stemmed red roses we placed over his heart and the golf club we wedged under his arm.

We sat and meditated for quite awhile. When we opened our eyes, there was a little kitten a few feet in front of us batting a string as if to say: life goes on. It was so innocent! So precious. We realized how true it was and how precious every single moment of our life is, and how fleeting.

While we were waiting for the ashes, we decided to go to the Kansas City TM facility to visit with the people there. We wanted to hear about my father's last days since he was with them on a meditation course when he died. They were surprised to see us and gave me a long emotional hug. As we talked, they told me the beautiful stories of his last days.

Ravi was very close to my father because he taught him the advanced TM Sidhi course. Although there were many people on the course, he had to teach my father separately because my dad was hard of hearing. So he met with him every day, and they developed a close bond.

When my dad had his aneurysm and was dying he put a note outside his door that said: "I need help." Ravi's wife, Priya, saw the note when walking down the hallway and rushed into his room. Priya called an ambulance because my father appeared very gray looking.

When the ambulance arrived they brought a gurney for him but, because of the winding staircase at the Kansas City facility, they couldn't get the gurney around the stairs. So they sat him in a gold velvet high backed chair and carried him down the red-carpeted staircase. Priya said it was like they were carrying a king. It had a very regal feeling to it. On the way down the stairs he told Priya how fulfilled he was and thanked her and Ravi for everything. He told her how happy he was that he fulfilled his daughter's desire for him to get the Sidhis. He couldn't be happier or more fulfilled.

Then she said he turned white as a sheet. His voice changed to a very low ancient-sounding voice, and he spoke what she called a benediction to her. He said,"Priya, I bless you and your family and your family's family for generations to come. I bless you with prosperity and good health, great fortune, and long life with all the riches of heaven and earth".....She said he went on and on in the most eloquent manner. She said it was the most striking blessing she had ever heard and she was utterly moved.

When they got down the stairs, they laid him on the gurney and wheeled him out the door and into the ambulance. Once in the ambulance, he sat up and put his hands in the Namaste position and turned to Priya and said,"Namascara" and then he laid down, and they closed the ambulance door.

Ravi was upstairs watching from the classroom window where the last tape of the course was playing. He said. "If you didn't believe in God you would have been spooked because the whole time they were wheeling him out to the ambulance Maharishi was singing the puja and he finished just as they put him in the ambulance. Then there were a few seconds of silence, and then the taped clicked off at the exact moment the ambulance door clicked shut."

Then the ambulance drove down the driveway for about 10 seconds. And stopped.

He was gone.

I sat in deep silence remembering my father. This story made me reflect deeply on his beautiful qualities. His countenance as a funeral director; all the people who told me, "Your father is a saint;" his depth and warmth; how, to this day, he is remembered for his gentle, loving kindness, his compassion, and his unarguable wisdom.

When we picked up the ashes, I was in for another surprise. They handed me a 1'x1'x1' cardboard box that was very heavy. I was stunned. I was unprepared for the eerie feeling that this was my father in that box.

In a bit of a stupor, I asked John what we should do with the box, and he replied, "Let's put your dad right here on the front seat between us!" With that, I snapped out of it and jumped into the front seat next to my dad and into the acceptance of my father's new status. We put the ashes between us on the seat, and down the road the three of us went!

After a few minutes, John started to speak quietly and thoughtfully about the realization he was having. He said, "This is a soul who has been planning his exit for a long time. He left his woman-friend in Wyoming and broke that attachment. Then he came to Fairfield to be with you. While he was there, your boyfriend kept you from being with him so he could start breaking his deep attachment to you. Then he came on this advanced TM course in Kansas City where he knew no one, and yet the group of people felt like family. He put himself in an environment of loving people that were not his family, so he was unattached. This allowed him to make his exit without anyone holding him back. If you had been with him, he couldn't have gone. His attachment to you was too great, and it would have held him back."

THAT resolved my second concern which was that I didn't get to spend as much time with him as I had wanted to while he was in Fairfield. It was then that I realized that my overly obsessed boyfriend played a big role in helping my father break his attachment to me. He would not allow us to be together as we naturally would have. He prevented us from getting even closer as his time of transition unknowingly approached.

At my father's funeral in Fairfield Iowa, in the old chapel there, many people from his Kansas City course got up to speak about him. Classmates shared remarkable stories about my father's integrity and character. Apparently, when they got to the course, a young man from Fairfield had forgotten something required for the course. He told how my father offered to drive back to Fairfield (five and a half hours) to get it for him with the same panache as going to the corner store to pick up a loaf of bread.

Finally, a man from India got up and said, "In my country, we call men of this stature a Saint. And the word Saint in my country is not used lightly. It is used very specifically. This man, I can tell you, was a Saint." When he finished, it was time for me to get up and tell the story of this saint and just what a great soul he was. As I was speaking, I knew that I was born to give his eulogy.

A couple of days later one of the students called me and told me of the surreal night he had had with my father the night before he died. He said that my dad sat next to him on the step outside and told him the whole story of his life.

This boy told me that he knew all about my family, my mother, my brothers, our growing up in Eau Claire, the funeral home, my divorce, how he never understood why I got a divorce, that he loved Scott like his own son, how he lived in and left Wyoming to be with me in Fairfield and on and on. He knew all my life stories, our family's life story. They spent an hour or so on that step, and when my dad got up to leave, the boy asked him. "So what's next for you Jacques?" and dad answered, "I'm going to find home again."

And that he did.

Those were his last spoken words.

We've probably all heard that just before someone dies their life flashes before them. Well, my dad's life flashed before him in this conversation with a near stranger the night before he died. His life was complete. He was going home. His entire life of loving open-heartedly through all things resulted in the most glorious exit from his body. It's hard to argue with that.

I finally understood why I wasn't there when he died—why I didn't hear the call of his soul beckoning me to be with him, to support and release him as he crossed over, holding his hand through his most sacred journey. He had to leave on his own terms, in his own way, so that his message would be indelibly imprinted across his face in death, exquisitely lit so it couldn't be missed. For me. So I would behold his message and forever change the way I live my life. And so I would share his message with you today.

At every given moment…we have the choice…to love open-heartedly…or not

and when we get to the end of our life…it's all going to add up to the choices we made at every given moment.

46

DEATH IS NOT DEAD

"Sarah is a witch now."

That was the opening line of a story Ryan wrote about a middle-aged housewife experimenting with various persona searching for herself. I still remember that story because its message of how we change had such an impact on me.

The passion with which he wrote mirrored his deeply insightful and philosophical mind.

He was the editor of the school newspaper at the same time I was editor of the yearbook. Although I was a year younger, we had many reasons to interact and got along famously. Ryan had a core group of friends who also became my friends. I was admitted into his fold and Ryan, Seth, Jason, Charles, and I hung out a lot. Seth and I even dated for a while.

When I went to college, I found half the gang already there. Ryan, Jason, and Charles had a house together, and it quickly became the gathering place on campus. They threw big parties and my roommate Vickie and I always topped the guest list.

Ryan and I were inseparable. He never wanted me to pass out on the floor at his parties like everyone else did so he always insisted I sleep in his bed. We slept together, platonically, throughout college. As you might imagine, we became very close friends. We had great fun together, we had each other's back, and enjoyed long talks deep into the night. We found out that we were simpatico in every respect; always had been and still were.

After college Ryan was shipped off to Australia with the Navy and I never heard from him after that. Meanwhile, the rest of us partied like animals, and Ryan's friend Jason remained in Oshkosh even after he graduated.

In my third year of college, I decided I'd had enough partying. I wanted to buckle down and study. But I was so entrenched in my partying lifestyle that I knew the only way I would be able to make the change would be to leave my friends and switch schools. So I escaped.

Since my parents had moved to Colorado, the University of Northern Colorado in Greeley became my school of choice.

Once in Colorado and packed to go to my new school, my brother Mike and his friend John took me out to celebrate my send off. We settled into the "Three Brothers" bar stools and started drinking shots of tequila. Some say tequila is considered a drug, not alcohol. True or not there is something dreamy about tequila and the euphoria it creates. It's a little trippy. As the shot glasses hit the bar, one after another, and the lemons flew into my mouth just as fast, my mind started on this "trip." At one point I "realized" I had to go to Australia to visit my friend Ryan. I had to. It was a clear realization.

When I told John my plan he "realized" he had to go too! I guess he must have had the same number of shots as me!

We decided that since he had money and I had a car, we would leave the next day. The plan was to drive to California, get on a boat and work our way to Australia. Voila!

Simple. Right?

Well, guess again!

I got home about 4 AM and immediately headed for the basement apartment to wake up my brother Marty. I needed to recruit his help explaining this to mom and dad.

"Marty wake up!"

"What time is it?"

"It's 4 o'clock."

"In the morning?"

"Yes. I need your help!"

"But Margo, it's 4 O'clock in the morning!" And he pulled the covers over his head and rolled over.

"Marty listen to me. I need your help. I am going to Australia today!"

He half opened one eye. "What?"

"I'm going to Australia. TODAY."

"Well, Australia will still be there when I wake up."

"No, I'm leaving this morning. I don't know how to tell

mom and dad."

Apparently, the urgency registered because he pulled himself up, sat back against the wall, unglued his eyelids by rubbing them open and looked at me with a contorted look. "Well don't tell them the way you just told me! Why are you going to A U S T R A L I A? "

"I need to see Ryan. John and I are driving to California, getting on a boat and working our way over to Australia."

"So you are going to Australia just to see Ryan?"

"Yes."

"Why?"

"I need to see him."

"Why does John need to see Ryan? Does he even know him?"

"No."

"Okay, let me get this straight. John is going with you to Australia so you can see this guy he doesn't even know. And you just need to see Ryan for no reason?"

"Yup, that's it. I just know I need to do this."

"But can't you just write him a letter?"

"No. I have to go. It's hard to explain!"

"It's going to be a lot harder to explain this to mom and dad."

"I know! That's why I need your help! I don't know how to tell mom and dad that I'm not going to college today….that I'm going to Australia instead of finishing school."

He finally heard my plea and helped me hatch a plan: "Just tell them!"

So I did. Later that morning I called my mom and dad into my bedroom and told them the news. My mother fell back on the bed and fainted. I thought she was just being dramatic, but she really did faint. My dad, on the other hand, didn't say a word. He stared deep into my eyes with huge thoughtfulness. He just stared for what seemed like a very long time. I looked back without even blinking. I was resolute. When my mom came to and sat back up, I told them I had to do this rather than finish college right now. They had no choice in the matter, and they knew it. I was going to Australia.

I must admit there was another reason churning deep inside me. We grew up with plenty of money, and I was used to that lifestyle. But since my parents moved to Colorado, it seemed like things were changing somehow. I feared that my father was losing his money. I kept asking my brothers," Is dad losing his money?" "Are we OK?" No one knew. Or at least no one told me. My dad certainly wouldn't tell me. I just sensed things were different and it scared me. Part of the motivation for this trip, besides having to see Ryan, was to find out if I could make it on my own should my fears be true. I didn't know if I could pay for my life if I had to, and it freaked me out to think about it. So I had to find out.

After I had packed the car to go, my father came out to me with a huge wad of cash rolled up in his hand and offered it to me. I said "No dad. I need to see if I can make it on my own." (I didn't have a dime to my name). He withdrew the money, looked intently into my eyes and deep into my soul. He knew this was a sojourn, and I was breaking away. His soft parting words to me," Mag, I hope you find what you are looking for." I grabbed him and cried…hard. We held each other for a long time. We didn't say another word. I got into my new light blue VW Bug and drove to pick up John.

Once in California, we stayed with a friend of John's who was also a classmate of my brother Mike's from Eau Claire named Terry. Terry was the older brother of Ryan's friend, Seth that I dated after high school. Terry was also a Vietnam Vet and had run into Mike in Viet Nam. They were both on backs of trucks going in different directions when they passed each other on the road. Terry recognized Mike and yelled," Lenmark!" "Terry!" Mike yelled back waving his helmet. It was a surprise moment of friendship in the middle of a war. One word and then they rumbled down the road and out of sight. A gift in the middle of a sweltering and dangerous jungle.

To book our passage to Australia, I called every boat company in LA and then on the entire west coast and found the same answer. Not only was there a 1-year waiting list to board but once on the boat, we would not be able to get off in Australia. We had to stay on the boat all the way back to the U.S. We couldn't hitch a ride to Australia after all! What were we thinking? After thousands of miles to get here, we hadn't even researched our plan, and now we find out it wasn't even possible! Oh—the ignorance of youth!

I must say there is a beauty in that crazy youthful spontaneity. Such innocent thinking leads you down a path you would never consider once the rational mind kicks in. Just jump straight in and see what happens! Well, what happened is our tequila induced plan fell flat on its face, and we consequently found ourselves living in LA. I felt a big setback in not getting to surprise Ryan with a visit. But I also gulped realizing I now faced the real-life challenge of supporting myself.

I set out to join the workforce. Luckily, I was hired right away by Avis-Rent-A-Car at LAX (LA airport) where Terry worked. The fun part about that job was keeping a "Stardust" list as we were directly in the path of all the stars as they exited their planes. My most memorable evening was renting a car to Don Knots. Hard to mistake that nose and smile! He was my favorite. He was as funny and friendly in person as you would expect from seeing him on screen. I felt we could have been buddies, given the chance. This was before the age of crowd-crushing paparazzi. Or maybe he was just more incognito than the rest. Or humbler.

We often saw movie scenes being filmed close by as we worked. It was an exciting "glam" job and considered a bit prestigious to be working at LAX.

Worried my salary would not be enough to live on, I took a second job as manager of a nearby bar. My regulars would put a quarter in the jukebox and play "Maggie May" for me every single night. It made me feel like I was home. I got to know their usual drinks and would surprise them every once in a while with something new I'd conjured up or learned from my recipe book. We had a good time. I liked them and liked the job. The more social I was, the more fun I had and the more money I made.

John and I lived with Terry for several months. I felt comfortable with Terry because he reminded me so much of his brother Seth. Such a nice guy, fun, charming, and good looking. He had that big Norwegian smile. After some time, Terry and I hooked up, and we moved into our own place. We started out having a lot of fun together, going to crazy parties, and making new friends. It was exciting.

My first introduction to California parties was a potluck drug party. As everyone came through the door, they threw their pills into a bowl and then everyone would grab out of the bowl. It was insane. Waaaay insane. No one knew what they were on, many were freaking out and no one knew how to help them. I just sat in the corner watching the most bizarre scene I'd ever witnessed, having no interest in participating in such madness.

Terry and I both worked at Avis but on different shifts. Terry worked the night shift, and I worked the day. That schedule started to wear on us. By the time he got home from work I was already in bed, and by the time I got home he was already gone. When I did see him he was always tired because he came home, smoked dope til late, then slept all day. We were in different worlds. He bought me a dog so I would have a companion while he was gone and have protection. She was a beautiful white fluffy sheepdog we named Panda.

Terry, though a fun guy, would often burst out in unprovoked anger which I never understood. Today I realize it was Posttraumatic Stress Disorder from his time in Viet Nam. But with no understanding of what it was at the time or what to do about it, it wore me down. We no longer got along. We seemed to be sliding quickly down a steep slope with nothing to catch us.

One night while Terry was at work, I decided to smoke a joint by myself which was something I had never done. I rarely smoked to begin with, but if I did, it was always done socially, never alone. The grass he had was Jamaican flower tops and very potent; I rolled a fat joint and smoked the whole thing.

The room became visually distorted and wavy and then almost disappeared. I felt immovable in my chair but somehow managed to get myself into the bathroom. Standing in front of the mirror I had a strange hallucination which took an interesting turn. My face became the hub of a wheel. All around it in a big circle came the faces of every one of my previous boyfriends. Each face was joined to the hub by a spoke. The spoke was the quality in each of them that had attracted me to them. After the circle was complete, out of the hub where my face had been, Ryan's face appeared. When that happened, I realized that he had every one of the qualities in each of the spokes. He had all the qualities of the perfect person for me and—in fact—he was the one for me. He was it. A rush of otherworldly knowing swept over me and filled me with a total sense of fulfillment. Every cell in my body was filled with glittery, sparkly light.

When I woke up in the morning, I had a completely different feeling about my life and Terry. I was no longer supposed to be with him. I was supposed to be with Ryan. My whole original reason for being here brought to light by my tequila trip, made perfect sense. Terry was clearly not the one for me, and I told him so. I asked him to move out, and he was devastated. Because we didn't have much money, he asked if he could stay with me until he found a place to live and that was fine with me.

Over the next weeks, I spent all my time thinking about Ryan and trying to write him a letter to explain what I had realized. But the words were not coming easily. It was such a transition from our great friendship to this huge realization that I just couldn't find the words to express it. Every day I wrote but to no avail. I went through reams of paper. I'd write, I'd rip it up, and throw it away. Next day I'd write again, rip it up, and throw it away. Day after day the same thing.

Finally one day it all came pouring out of me, like a fast flowing river, everything I felt and realized. I had found my voice, and it was perfect. I sent it off across the ocean. The postman told me exactly when it would arrive so I noted the date and waited for the day he would receive it.

When the highly anticipated day came, I was sitting in my kitchen. I can still remember it clearly. It was sunny; my kitchen was small and white; white cupboards, white paint, sweet and lovely. I was sitting at the kitchen table sipping chamomile tea, looking out the window, imagining Ryan getting my letter. I was sitting quietly with my eyes closed trying to sense if I could actually feel when he was reading it. My heart was beating fast in anticipation, wondering how long I would have to wait for a response, and more importantly what it would be.

A sudden clunk pulled me out of my reverie. I heard the mail drop through the slot in the front door onto the wooden floor. Along with the letters was a distinct sound of a heavier package. I quickly went over to pick up the mail to see what the package was. It was from Australia! I ripped it open to find a cassette tape from Ryan.

I ran into the bedroom, scrambling through the closet as quickly as I could, tossing clothes and shoes to get to the cassette player on the floor. I couldn't imagine what music he had sent me. I clicked the tape into place, closed the cover, and sank into the nearest stuffed chair and closed my eyes. I was ready to enjoy his beautiful gift, hoping he was reading my letter as I listened to his music, amazed at the timing of it all.

"Margo, I have gone through tablets of government-issued paper, and just as many government-issued pens and haven't been able to express to you what I need to say. I simply cannot find the words. So I've decided to say it to you instead. "I have had a deep unexplainable realization that you are the one for me. I realize this may sound crazy. I know we've been friends…so long…please hear me…if you feel…..…mutual…..….hope…….….someday."

I could barely hear anything he said after the first sentence. I remember a blur of his feelings for me…I was the one for him…he hoped it was reciprocal…or could become so…he couldn't wait to see me again….home at Christmas….deep love…..…inspired…….….excited……our life. I can't remember anything else. And nothing else mattered. It was surreal. It synthesized into an epiphany of confirmation, and I could hardly breathe. I sat there in a state of euphoria for I don't know how long after listening to that tape. I'm sure he was reading my letter at the same moment and feeling the same thing. He had to be as blown away as I was. I knew we were sharing this unbelievable moment.

When I could finally breathe again, my life was crystal clear. I decided to let Terry stay in our house, and I moved back to Colorado. I wanted to be near my parents for a while and then go back to finish school in Oshkosh, so I'd be there when Ryan got out of the Navy at Christmas. Terry was angry and upset, but I couldn't help it. I had to go, and I did.

I moved to Colorado Springs and found a job at a high-end restaurant. Panda and I got an apartment, and I was looking forward to making some money and getting back to Wisconsin. My job was going well. I liked it. I made a lot of money waitressing. It was a busy place and my new friends and I were having a great time. I couldn't remember being happier.

One day after several weeks on the job, I was called to the front to take care of a customer. It turns out…it was Terry!

I hadn't been in touch with him and didn't give him my phone number or address on purpose. He had gotten violent in the past, especially when I left, and I wanted nothing to do with him anymore. So I was shocked when he showed up at my workplace. I don't know how he found me.

He was having a hard time. He didn't have any money, he'd lost his job, and he wasn't doing well. So I let him stay with Panda and me. I had him give me a security deposit and pay half the rent which he agreed to do. I made it clear to him that I would never get back together with him. He understood and signed my lease.

It didn't take long for his violence to flare up as his drinking escalated. This time he put his hand through a wall of the apartment. I asked him to leave. I couldn't take anymore.

A few days later he called to get his security deposit back, and I refused, telling him I needed the money to fix the wall. He got so enraged that he told me, in scary expletives, that he was coming over the next day at 2 o'clock in the afternoon and if I didn't have his money, I would be very sorry. I froze. He was a vet. Between his temper and having killed people in Viet Nam, I didn't know the extent to which his mental state was capable.

I was petrified. My brother Mike would know how to deal with Terry. He was living an hour away in Pueblo West. I immediately called him. He was concerned and said he'd handle the situation with Terry for me, and not to worry. I could tell though that he was. They were fellow vets, and they had seen each other in Viet Nam so there was built-in respect that should play in our favor.

Mike arrived around noon the next day in case Terry changed his mind and showed up early. We waited outside the house. Exactly at 2 o'clock, we saw Terry coming toward the house. He seemed his usual friendly self, big smile, but I noticed his eyes were wild, like in the cartoons when a madman's eyes are depicted with moving circles. Mike saw it too. His eyes were fast-moving circles of madness. He was out of his mind. Mike ordered me into the house.

He whispered for me to go upstairs and hide. I ran upstairs and hid behind the bathroom door making myself as thin as possible so as not to be seen if Terry walked by looking for me. I heard Mike invite Terry into the house. As Terry walked in, I heard Mike try to reason with him. I heard their voices get louder, I heard talk of money, I heard reasoning from Mike, and then a big scuffle and both of them were on the floor. I was consumed with fear…panic-stricken…and aware of the grave danger Mike and I were both in. Terry was a big guy, and he was MAD. I thought he would kill Mike!

Suddenly it was quiet, and I didn't know what had happened… and I didn't dare open the door to find out. I heard nothing. Were they both dead? I didn't know who was where or what had happened to either of them. Then I heard footsteps upstairs, and my blood froze. I stopped breathing so he couldn't hear me. But my heart was pounding so hard I feared he could hear it. In a few seconds, I heard my brother's voice, "Margo?" "Mike!" I collapsed in his arms in relief and sobbed. He held me tight. "He won't come back," he assured me. He took me over to the bathroom window, and we both watched as Terry walked away. After about half a block he turned around and started to come back! As Mike started for the bathroom door, Terry whistled for Panda, and she ran to him, wagging her tail. Then he turned and walked away with her. I can still see them walking down the street away from my house. He had managed to put a knife in my heart after all by taking my beloved dog!

But I knew that he needed her more than I did.

To this day I can still see that poignant scene in my mind. Terry and Panda walking away. Panda unconditionally trotting down the sidewalk, vigorously wagging her tail alongside her master. Her master lost and alone except for her. I was happy he had her.

I went back to Oshkosh as planned. I was now in my last year of college, having taken an interesting year off. My friends had all graduated, so I rented an apartment with all new people who I didn't know very well, and I was ready to study! I was back on track, making straight A's as I had in high school. I was counting the months and now the weeks until Ryan's return from Australia.

It was early December, and Ryan was due home for Christmas. I was overcome by a strong urge to call his parents and find out exactly what day he would be home so I could make plans to see him over the holidays. His brother answered the phone. He didn't know exactly when he would be home and went to get his mother so I could ask her. After a few minutes, I heard

…Ryan's voice.

"Wha…what are you…doing…home?" I stammered. "They gave me an early release, and I just walked through the door. I wanted to surprise you."

I was in shock! He was home. Already. And for good.

He immediately made plans to come and see me in Oshkosh.

I was excited and full of anticipation. The last time I saw him we were just friends. So much had happened since then with no communication except the cassette and my letter. I was pacing when I heard the knock on my apartment door.

When I opened the door, we just stared at each other as if adjusting our eyes to some mysterious apparition standing before us. Oddly, we hugged a pretty awkward hug and then I invited him in. It was strange. It felt so weird. It was uncomfortable. It felt like I was looking at a stranger. Here in the flesh stood my great friend and I didn't even know what to say to him. The game changed but the players didn't, and we no longer knew the rules. It was awkward right out of the box.

The feeling was that everything had taken place on some other level and to be together face-to-face felt unnatural—even though we had been such close friends for so many years. It's hard to explain the dichotomy of what I was feeling—like two divergent worlds colliding. It became clear that not only had the game changed but so had the players. In fact, we had changed a lot. It was difficult to bridge the gap. And yet here he was, my friend, my great friend. We had come to realize that we were "the ones" for each other. What could be so hard about that?

Our sudden, transformative and synchronized realizations compounded by the total lack of communication between us, made finding this new ground impossible. The gap between the old and the new was too wide. I always thought I was a good communicator, but I was at a total loss. Me more than him I think. I could not speak coherently. It was a strange meeting. He stayed overnight with his friend Jason who was still living in Oshkosh and left the next day. We both felt weird. It was confusing. It was very odd in light of what we had both experienced while he was away.

He never came back to Oshkosh.

A couple of weeks later I went to Eau Claire. We tried it again. We met at Mooney's Bar. We talked to each other, but it was awkward still. I know we were both wondering what was going on. Somehow we couldn't talk to each other anymore. I went back to his house with him and like we had done in college, I slept in his bed, but it was not romantic. In fact, unlike college, it felt awkward and unnatural. We were not communicating at all.

It was strained and strange. Even our friends were confused. Several visits to Eau Claire ended the same way. So I purposely did not go back for a while to see if time would help us out.

At Easter break, I decided to return to Eau Claire. It had been a couple of months since I'd seen Ryan. We had had no communication at all.

I ran into him at Mooney's. My brother Mark and his wife Judy were there, and I was sitting at a table with them. Ryan sat down next to Mark and started to talk to him. I soon realized that everything he was saying to Mark was actually a message to me. Mark realized it too. At that point, I began responding to his indirect comments by speaking back to him through Mark. It was effective. I learned a lot in that conversation. I learned that he still had feelings for me. He learned that I did too. We both heard how uncomfortable we were and that neither of us understood why. The conversation became entertaining. It worked. We were gaining steam. We were both able to say things through Mark that we couldn't say to each other. We were laughing and enjoying saying all kinds of things to each other that we wanted each other to know. My heart was feeling light for the first time since he got home. I was starting to feel myself again.

After Mark and Judy left, he asked me to come back to his house, and I did. It was late, so he started to walk me upstairs to go to bed. I stopped.

"What's the matter?"

"I'm not going."

"Why?"

"Because every time we go up there, we lose communication."

He stopped dead in his tracks. He knew exactly what I was saying.

He started back down the stairs. He took my hand and sat me down on the couch. He looked straight into my eyes.

"OK. Let's lay all our cards on the table".

We both sat back on the couch as we pulled card after card from our hearts and laid them face up on the table. We started from the beginning in college, and discussed every nuance of experience leading up to the "big revelation." We laid out every single feeling we'd had since then, why it was so hard to talk, and pondered the understandable chasm that had emerged between us. Our minds simply could not reconcile our college friendship with our otherworldly revelation. It was a profound, life-changing experience that created an unnatural condition on his return. We just hadn't been able to bridge the gap.

But we did by four in the morning!

With all the cards on the table, we were light as feathers! Everything had finally come together, and that realization across the seas finally came to fruition. Our hearts were flowing, and we were in love just as sure as we had been when he sent the tape and I sent the letter.

We walked upstairs, and this time the communication was perfect. At one point, I had an inner experience that "This is it. This is perfection. Beyond this there is nothing." It transcended everything in the physical world. It was beyond the realms of love as we know it. It was an experience of perfection like I'd never known could exist.

A flow of euphoria in dreamlike proportions.

We woke up in the morning in bliss.

We were floating.

I sat in his back yard, and the sun had an extra shine on. I watched him through the sliding glass doors making eggs for our breakfast and thinking "there has never been a more perfect moment in all of creation!" If heaven existed on earth, this was it. We were in heaven. It was Easter Sunday, our stone had been rolled away, and we were free.

We talked about our life together. How fun it will be with all our mutual friends, our families, our own family…and all of it was mutual.

We decided I would come back soon to plan our wedding.

For some reason, I decided not to go back to Eau Claire to see Ryan the weekend we had planned. Something came up at school, so we both decided to wait a couple of weeks.

That Friday night I went to the bar with my roommates. We were drinking shots of—yes—tequila! I hadn't done that since the night with my brother and John in Colorado. I was sure I wouldn't decide to go to Australia again because I didn't have any reason to anymore. My reason was right here creating his new life with me! Certain moments can make you realize how much has changed and drinking tequila shots was that moment for me. The shots brought me to Ryan the first time. This time as I drank them I celebrated that he was here—with me—forever.

Amidst all the fun we were having I suddenly felt something freeze inside and my heart tighten. I wondered if I was having a heart attack. The pain, the short breath. My mind went blank, and everyone in the room, all the sounds, the laughter, the noise faded into the background. I could barely hear anything. I could see the room full of people laughing and drinking, but I couldn't hear them. I had no thoughts. I looked at the clock, and the clock was frozen too. Time stood still. Was I having a heart attack? A stroke? Wasn't I too young for these things? I sat still. Not even a twitch. Everything stopped, and I was frozen in time.

I stared blankly into this strange silence for a long time. I did nothing. Then I asked for a drink. When I got it, I chugged it. Then I asked for another, and I chugged that one too. And yet another. I'd never done that before. These were drinks, not shots. Straight alcohol, no rocks. I ignored my friends' pleas to stop. I drank one after another. I was oblivious. I got off the bar stool and didn't remember how I got home, but when I did, I passed out on my bed fully clothed.

Meanwhile, Ryan and three of our friends went to this happening bar outside Eau Claire. Doc and the Interns were playing at the bar that night, and they always drew a huge crowd. The band raised the crowd to their feet early on, and by the end of the night, everyone was on the dance floor. It was a fun evening! The last dance had everyone, Ryan and his friends included, dancing to the Doobie Brothers' "Long Train Running." It was the last song before lights out at the tavern.

The crowd filed out of the bar, laughing, staggering, yelling their good nights to each other. They'd had a great time.

I heard a distant sound that I could barely make out as the phone ringing. It matched a ringing that I was hearing inside my head in my drunken dream. I was awakened, however, because the ringing wouldn't stop no matter how many times I pulled the pillow over my head to muffle the sound. It was a call from Jason. I could barely hear through my hangover. He was hysterical. He was crying so hard I couldn't understand him. "Jason. Slow Down!" I only made out a couple of his broken, staggering words: "Ryan" and "killed." I have no idea what else he said to me in that phone call.

Ryan and his friends had piled into their car after leaving the bar. Soon after exiting the parking lot, they crossed the railroad tracks. The driver never saw the oncoming train. They were broad-sided by a long train running. All were killed instantly except the driver. The car was totaled, and Ryan was dead.

It was all happening when I "froze" on the barstool.

Instantly, my mind was transported to another place. I was outside myself. I hadn't experienced shock before this. Jason picked me up, and we drove to Eau Claire and into the saddest town and the most gut-wrenching environment I'd ever known. This accident brought the whole town to its knees as these friends had been some of the most popular guys in town, loved and connected to everyone. It was emotional devastation.

There was no one unaffected by this tragedy. Everyone, the friends, the families, the whole town was immersed in pain. Their hearts shredded, staring in disbelief, grabbing their chests, tear-stained faces, holding each other, pooled together in grief. Everyone in town had lost their friends.

My friends would break down in my arms when they saw me. Somehow out of nowhere, I became the strong one. I found myself saying things to them that made them feel better. I knew some truth suddenly. When I saw his body lying in the casket, I knew he was not in there. He was with me. I could feel him. I was in total communication with him. Every time someone would say something to me I would respond to them with wisdom and truth that deeply moved and comforted them. I turned out to be a comfort to everyone around town and at the funeral. It was wonderful for them and also for me. My brother Mark said to me, "Margo it's like Ryan is talking through you." and he was. Everything I said during that time was the truth about Ryan and where he was now. I wish I had recordings of what I said because it was all coming to me from Ryan. And people knew it. They couldn't argue with anything I was saying.

During the funeral, I struggled over whether I should stand up and tell the pastor he was wrong. That Ryan was not dead. That nothing he was saying had any truth or relevance. But I decided not to. He was doing what he was trained to do, and it was helping people just to hear his words, no matter what they were. It's hard to know a deeper truth when you are not in the same space, looking for the same thing as someone else. It was Ok. I listened to what he had to say, and I respected it. I was with Ryan, and I was happy with that. In fact, I was in bliss, balanced, grief-free, and all-knowing. We were in total communication just like the last time I saw him alive. In a sense, nothing had changed. I was fine, and so was he.

The funerals took place in separate funeral homes on different days so everyone could attend them all. At the funeral of our friend, Seth, the former boyfriend of mine, I ran into…Terry. You can imagine, it was bittersweet. Both because it was his brother's funeral, and because it was my boyfriend's funeral, the one for whom I had left him. Also because the last time I saw Terry, it was a bad scene which now seemed all the more trivial in light of why we were both here. We were joined in a bitter, mutual, strange and tragic loss together. What a sad reunion. What a sad reason to have to see him again. For both of our sakes. We didn't say too much. We just cried. There was nothing to say except we were sorry. For so many reasons.

I never saw Terry after that. I never really thought about him again. But it turns out this whole horrific experience somehow silenced him. He couldn't cope with it. He stopped talking and ended up in a hermit-like situation and didn't speak a word for 30 years. Thirty years later, when he came out of it, one of his first calls was to me. I still recognized his voice. "Margo. This is Terry. I owe you an apology." Can you imagine? THIRTY YEARS later! I had nothing but forgiveness for him. I always had forgiveness in my heart for him. I forgave him the moment I saw him walk away with my dog. Panda forgave him too as she wagged her tail all the way down the street when they walked away.

So in my mind, there was never a need for an apology. But the respect I have for someone who would do that...admit everything and take the time all those years later to track me down to apologize, is beyond words. He is a gentleman...and a hero. I wish the government would call him and apologize for getting him into that war in the first place. The pain it must have created to cause all that anger. Such a good human being with so much to offer. His ambition crushed and rolled into a joint and dumped into a drink only to choke the life force right out of his spirit... turning his beautiful Norwegian smile into a violent rage. His joy ripped from him; his future robbed. He's the one who deserves the apology, not me.

I gave him the highest Medal of Honor that day. That is a mark of a true hero.

A couple of weeks after all the funerals I crashed.

My high balanced state of grace came thundering down around me like a tsunami. It was like someone had dropped me out of an airplane and I fell to the ground and had no idea where I was. I was lost. I was depressed, and I couldn't pull myself out of it. I went to Ryan's house and slept in his bed. I took one of his t-shirts with me and slept with it so I could smell him. I went to my brother Mark's for a few weeks but couldn't stand what a burden I had become on everyone.

So I went back to Oshkosh. I didn't know what to do. I couldn't work. All I wanted to do was sit by a stream, like

Thoreau, until I figured out the meaning of life and death. I had to know the reason for death, or life would never hold any meaning for me again.

I started visiting churches. I went to one church after another but didn't find my answers. I even tried the Holy Rollers. I listened to people speaking in tongues. I tried to understand what they were saying to one another, tried to understand what they knew that I didn't. Everyone was trying their hardest to save me, and I needed saving. Desperately.

I picked up a book that my father had given me called Cosmic Consciousness by Allen Buck. I read the passage about John the Baptist riding on a donkey, and suddenly something shot through me like an arrow piercing an apple on my head. The passage explained how he had experienced cosmic consciousness. I had just started TM a couple of months before reading this, and my teacher had explained a phenomenon called cosmic consciousness.

While reading this passage, I realized that Christ was in a state of consciousness that was higher than mine, much higher, but that I could also reach a higher state of consciousness. I realized that consciousness is a state of awareness that can grow—and does. Continually. It made sense because life is always growing; everything is growing. The seed sprouts and grows into a tree; the tree blossoms and then fades and drops its leaves and dies, but meanwhile it drops another seed, and the cycle continues. This was a huge realization. It was what I was trying to grasp during my entire life growing up with my dad. I just now realized what it all meant and what the goal of all spiritual quests is. It is about growth of consciousness.

It was an enormous realization.

We are on a journey…a journey of souls if you will. We travel through life, together and apart, for the growth of our consciousness, toward greater understanding, and toward the greatest love. A journey seeking oneness with our Creator and a willingness to "let thy will be done." It all comes together in the end, and we travel this journey together, this journey of souls. John the Baptist's donkey ride revealed it to me! I felt so alive! Things were coming together. My answers were coming!

Later that day I opened a letter from one of my best friends. The letter began, "I am sorry to hear about Ryan, but I am happy to hear you've started TM. It's the fastest way to relieve suffering in the world." I had started TM in March but stopped when Ryan died in May. And now, after reading that letter, I decided to put it to the test. I was suffering, and I needed help. I was about to prove whether what she said was true or not. I put TM to the test starting right then.

I sat down and meditated that very afternoon. I meditated twice a day for 20 minutes, as taught, without fail from that afternoon on. From the first meditation, I began to feel some relief from the pain, the next meditation, more relief; after a week of this twice daily practice I started to feel myself again. I was digging out. I was taking one step at a time emerging from a deep dark hole. Every day I took another step, and every day I felt a little better, a little lighter, and a little more alive.

Until one day…I stepped out into the full sunshine. I was out, and I was free! It was nothing short of a miracle! Between my recent revelation and my transcending experience, I had a whole new lease on life. My paradigm and my experience matched. I was complete. I realized that Ryan's death did for me what Christ did for all humankind. It set me free. It was my God-given birthright, delivered by grace, through love.

Not the romantic love that most people know as emotion. But love as pure life force; as the vital essence that we are born with, and that keeps us alive. It is the power and the glory that creates everything in this unfathomable universe that we inhabit. It's the love that all great religions reference. It is our deliverance. It delivered me. And provided me the answers I so desperately sought.

I realized something about death that made me understand life. Death is just a charade. Death is not dead. What appears to us as death is brilliant life unseen by us. There is only a succession of lives in a continuum of life. There is no death. Only change. Ryan's death made me realize that. When I saw his face and saw that he was not in his body, yet he was there with me, I knew he was still alive on some level. I realized that his life is continuing. It may be out of my reach at the moment, but he will return to me someday, in some yet unknown way, and we will be together again in this continuance we call life.

I now knew that everything in life happens for a reason. That every experience takes us to a higher place. It's the nature of life to give us more. More happiness, more awareness, more love, more understanding, more light, more knowledge, more God, more ourselves, more everything. My heart was at peace in this knowing.

Thoreau and I. We found our answers.

There is an evolution of the soul through higher states of consciousness, through many lives, many forms, and many incarnations. I was feeling rather euphoric again—not from tequila this time—but from a God-realized truth that opened my eyes to the continuum of life.

A gift from Ryan.

Another flow of euphoria in illuminating proportions.

A PAIN WORSE THAN DEATH

She was striking.

She stood so beautifully in front of us that I dare say—she was a vision. Her long white dress with a multi-nuanced purple and blue starburst that spanned its whole length, her blonde hair pulled into a French roll with blue glitter sprinkled throughout as if stars had fallen from the sky into her hair, her earrings sparkling in the artificial light, her radiant smile captivating the whole auditorium of people. It was her moment to shine, and she shone brightly. It was our family's moment to be proud of her, and we were.

We have all known them—The Supernovas. The Rock Stars. The Talented. The Beautiful. The ones whose lives create brilliance in ours just by their being. But then they implode. They burn out—and are gone—too soon.

That was my mother.

She shined. From the inside out. She was popular and well known in our community. She was a chairwoman of many committees, a leader of charity events, President of the Woman's Club, a fund-raiser for the church and the poor, always engaged, always gracious, always impressive.

But she had something eating at her, something we could

never understand. Loneliness, insecurity, DNA, who knows? Whatever it was it drove her to drink. We could overlook the small inconveniences her alcoholic episodes caused when we were young because the rest of her was so beautiful that we were mesmerized by her. Everyone was.

My mother would model for a local fashion store called "The Fashion Store," and she always treated every walkway like a runway. On Sunday mornings she would turn heads as she walked the church aisle, modeling her couture dresses and matching large brimmed hats. One foot in front of the other, her million dollar smile lighting up the sanctuary. There was always a spotlight on her.

She was larger than life.

One night my family was dining late at a popular Eau Claire restaurant. I was staring out the window at the cars going by pretending that everything outside the restaurant was a silent movie. My movie was abruptly interrupted however when a man at the table next to us got up and signaled for us to come with him. It was 10 PM, and he was opening his store for my mother so she could buy some shoes. They struck up a conversation between our two tables and the next thing you know, we were all going shopping!

Mom had a particularly soft spot in her heart for the poor. She often raised money and gave anything she could find or buy to create a better life for them. I guess she never took her fortunate life for granted.

When I was in sixth grade, I came home from school to

find my mom packing the car with boxes of clothes. On top of one of them, I spotted two of my favorite blouses; one was brand new. I blurted, "Mom what are you doing?"

"A family from the church has a daughter your size, and she needs them."

"But mom those are my favorite blouses!"

"I know honey; I will buy you some more. She needs them more than you do."

"But mom they…"

"Honey!" Which was her way of telling me the conversation was over, and off she went with my clothes.

Over the years we got used to it. We ended up with a horse in our backyard because she had given a poor woman from our church some money. The money was intended as a gift, but the woman insisted on repaying her. So, many years later, this poor woman deposited her white stallion in our corral insisting, against my mother's will, that she repay her somehow.

Many people in our town have my mother's name written in their hearts.

She was an extraordinary party planner. She would host birthday parties for us with elaborate decorations and so many prizes that no one would go home empty-handed. She made heart-shaped cakes for us to take to school on Valentine's day. She would peek her head into our classroom, and our friends would start whispering how pretty she was.

She is the one you'd hang out with for fun, the shoulder you'd cry on, the nucleus of our fun and the neighborhood "mom." Our friends would show up at our door asking to see our mother rather than us! They'd spend hours in the back room laughing and telling stories. We'd hear outbursts of giggling that would turn into fits of thigh-slapping laughter as she told story after story. I guess we missed a lot by hating her drinking and cutting her out of our lives when she did.

Mom was the life of every party—singing, dancing, laughing—and smack dab in the middle of every story. We liked attending our parent's parties just to watch her in the limelight! She was fun and exciting.

Her magnetism drew everyone in—like honeybees to nectar. But unfortunately for me, this golden bee could sting. With me, her light could turn dark on a dime.

In a Jekyll and Hyde sort of way, in some moment of exuberant fun, the fatal arrow would strike me straight in the heart. In front of my friends, her friends, my family, my boyfriends, at home, out to dinner, at my birthday parties, at any point when I least expected it. BAAM! My bubble would burst like an explosion loud enough for everyone to hear. I was embarrassed to death and humiliated in front of whoever was there. But then—just like it never happened— I bounced back. Completely normal. My recovery was so fast that people probably wondered if it happened or if they only imagined it. The truth is, it happened so often that I became well trained in denial.

Well into one of our famous parties, my mother's animated gestures caught my attention from across the room. I had just walked in from outside, and I saw her standing in the corner talking to a couple of my friends. But something was askew. Everyone was laughing and looked to be having a great time, but I noticed she was talking louder than usual and standing closer to the girls than normal. I saw her hand reach for the edge of the table, her slight stumble, her autocorrect, and then, as if nothing had occurred, she was back to storytelling. I prayed that I was the only one who noticed.

Growing up, our family tried to ignore these moments. We were her kids, and we adored her. She was our beauty queen, rock star hero, leader of our tribe and life of the party! Alcohol was just the sideshow and our little secret. As far as we were concerned, she could remain in the spotlight forever. But that night she faltered, something shifted. Her tiara slipped a little. I foresaw trouble. I don't know if anyone else saw it, but I ached with the foreshadowing of times to come.

But that moment passed.

Despite all of this, I would say that I had what most would consider a storybook childhood. My parents were a huge vortex that drew constant fun and excitement into our world. They befriended our friends which resulted in a revolving door of companions, and all the fun was at our house!

They allowed my brothers and me to have huge parties and would help orchestrate them down to the last detail. A few of our close friends formed an awesome band called the "Vandels," and they played at all of our parties. They were so good that my mom tried to get them on the Johnny Carson Show!

My brothers also had friends in bands, the most popular being "Doc and the Interns." One night my parents invited both bands to play at our house, and we set up two stage areas in our front yard in the country. Our huge gang of friends enjoyed their very own private rock festival with the best rock 'n' roll around!

One night, while we were sleeping, our house burned almost to the ground. Miraculously, our dog awakened us all, and everyone made it out. We lost everything but our picture albums and our home movies. Sneaking back into what was left of our house, my mom and I waded through popped popcorn and melted lava lamps to what used to be our bedrooms. She found charred bits of her mink coat, and I found a white lump of something that I later discerned to be my polyester prom dress.

The fire happened right before my 16th birthday, and I was feeling down because my mother could not host her usual extravaganza for this important day. Another year might not have meant so much, but sweet 16 seemed significant. As an alternative offering, my parents decided to take me to the country club for dinner. Dinner at six for six. Well,…OK…it was…nice. Despite their efforts to cheer me up and much seemingly forced conversation, I was still feeling glum.

After dinner, we went downstairs to check out the remodel

of the banquet hall just below the restaurant where we ate. My dad opened the door and walked in first. I followed him into the dark room. I thought he was looking for the light switch when suddenly bright lights and 50 friends exploded in front of me, "SURPRISE!" And I burst into tears!

My parents had seated me facing away from the golf course. While we were having dinner and forced conversation, the "Vandels" and their band equipment were being transported down the hill behind me to the banquet hall in golf carts. So were 50 friends! Apparently, there was a lot of silent commotion, and my parents and brothers watched the amusing show going on behind me through the entire dinner. They were especially amazed that I never had a clue about why they were talking so much and making up conversation to hold my attention. I did think it odd, but I just thought they were trying unsuccessfully hard to cheer me up.

To make this devastating birthday extra special my mother arranged a Hawaiian Luau theme for my party. Everyone dressed in Hawaiian floral shirts and dresses with leis. The country club catered the luau complete with chocolate covered ants! So, after feeling depressed on my 16th birthday, I ended up getting "leied" making this an extra sweet 16!

That was my mother who, despite her drinking and her fatal arrows, made me feel like the most important person in the world. She made everyone feel that way.

Every summer we'd move out to our cottage on Eau Claire Lake, with our dogs, cats and, since my mother had been a rodeo queen, all our horses. My dad only came to the lake on weekends because he had to run the funeral business. So, it was just my brothers, my mother, our menagerie and me.

Every day my brothers and I traveled in a pack, always looking for the next adventure and gathering as many kids on the lake to come with us as we could.

We spent our days skidding around the lake on water skis, jumping wakes, creating rooster tails and teaching all our friends how to ski. When we got tired of the water we'd head for the barn, grab our favorite horse and ride. Sometimes we would take the neighbor's big workhorse bareback into the water, climb up on her back, dive off, climb back up and do it again—for hours!

When our cousins Hank and Buzzy would drive 40 straight hours from Atlanta in their non-air-conditioned DeSoto to visit us, our cottage suddenly became the boys' camp.

One day my mom and her sister Helen were drinking their cocktails and catching up on life while mom made great strides knitting our ski sweaters. They heard a knock on the door and mom set her knitting needles on the table and answered the door. The eager couple asked if there were any rooms available. My mom incredulously responded, "This is a private home!" "But the sign says this is a resort," the husband retorted.

They walked to the top of our driveway where they indeed found signs that read, "Rathole's Resort" and "Hookface's Harbor" with arrows pointing toward our cottage. It took mom and Helen about two seconds to realize who had done that! My mother at first pretended to be upset and then burst out laughing. They all went across the street for a drink at Ken and Donna's Bar to enjoy how they'd been duped by the boy's camp.

No one was a stranger to my mother. But can you imagine someone wanting to stay at Rathole's Resort....on Hookface's Harbor?

Once at Ken and Donna's, my mom and Helen did their usual routine of singing and harmonizing and entertaining the guests at the bar. Mom was an expert at this. When my dad fought in the Second World War, mom enlisted in the WAC and entertained the troops by singing and dancing. So when faced with a crowd of eager people she couldn't help but entertain them. My cousin Hank recently retraced his footsteps back to the lake, and some of the locals still remember how mom and Helen would light up a room when they walked in.

And so the summer went on. The boys were making funeral home ink pens explode in the driveway. I was swimming and ambling bareback through the woods. Marty and the little neighbor girl were on their stick horses galloping around the neighborhood. And mom was knitting ski sweaters and drinking.

Oh! The cottage days. Those were the days my friend; we thought they'd never end! We were like Swiss Family Robinson with a ski boat and a band of horses!

But my storybook childhood was sprinkled with land mines

that my mother unwittingly planted on a regular basis.

Mom used to sunbathe with the Beatles blaring from speakers in the cottage. She had it turned up so we could hear it while swimming in the lake a mere 100 feet away. We played the record so much that it developed a skip. Every time it skipped you would hear my mother's command, "Get that record!" And someone would fly up the stairs into the cottage to move the needle. After a while, everyone would yell, "Get that record!" And no one would go, so it would continue skipping until it drove someone nuts enough to run up.

Coming back from the sand dunes one afternoon, we heard the record skipping, but mom wasn't sunbathing. We went upstairs. When we walked toward her bedroom, we found her lying motionless on the floor. We freaked! Breathless, we stepped back, our eyes like saucers. My brother Mike shook her many times, but she didn't move. Finally, he shook her real hard, and she barely opened her eyes and said," I took a nap" and closed her eyes again. Mike shooed everyone out of the room, and we ran out—scared to death and embarrassed that our friends saw her like that. Mike helped her onto the bed where she immediately passed out again.

That night we ate peanut butter and jelly sandwiches to which we had grown accustomed, but the night wasn't as much fun. Our nucleus was missing. And we were worried. She didn't wake up that night, and we didn't see her until late the next morning. We were relieved to see her, and we never told dad about the peanut butter and jelly sandwiches.

One Friday evening Dad arrived at the lake and couldn't find mom. He noticed the pontoon boat was gone, so he figured mom and her friend Nute had taken the boat out. After it had started to turn dark, he got concerned. He took our other boat out to look for them and found the pontoon floating at the far end of the lake, about to wash up on the shoreline. Mom and Nute were passed out in their lounge chairs, their cigarettes burned down to their fingers.

The disease was taking its toll.

If she wasn't entertaining our friends and relatives at our cottage, then she was hosting glamorous cocktail parties at our house. Mink stoles, bright red lipstick, martinis, Tommy Dorsey, loud chatter, and ashtrays full of cigarette butts.

At one of their parties, my mom asked me to play the piano for her friends. I hated it when she asked this of me, but of course, I did. I came out in my favorite outfit to impress her friends and make her proud. As soon as I walked into the living room, she implored of me—loudly enough to hush the entire party—"Go and change that hideous top!" I ran out of the room and heard her sheepishly apologizing to her friends for my appearance.

Soon she came into my room begging my forgiveness, but I wouldn't budge. Try as she might, she could not convince me to go back to the party or the piano. Her actions were hideous, not my top. The next day she came home with bags of gifts for me: a beautiful dress, new shoes, some ribbons for my hair. It worked. I gave in. We were OK again. We started chatting like school girls.

I could think of a million things she did to hurt me growing up if I hadn't blocked them out of my mind. When she flung her arrows at me, I instantly shut down, like a psychic freeze, but then, just as quickly, I would switch gears and pick right back up as if nothing had happened. Most of the details of the pain she inflicted escape me because I was truly not there. I would emotionally disappear, or I couldn't have survived. But the impact and its resulting scars remained.

Every time she hurt me she would beg my forgiveness with gifts. I was young and susceptible, so it worked. But there came a time when I could no longer be bought off. Perhaps she anticipated that. Maybe deep down inside she knew I'd be the one to blow the whistle on her drinking.

It was called "The Academy Awards" ceremony at our high school in Eau Claire, an annual event where the best student accomplishments were awarded trophies and plaques. Every year my mom was asked to give out the main award. It was a big deal in our town so The Fashion Store would dress her in their crowning glory to make this presentation.

So......the anticipated event was here…most of the awards were given out…and there she was.

A vision.

She stood so beautifully at the top of the staircase in her long white dress with the purple and blue multi-nuanced starburst; her hair pulled back into a French roll with blue glitter sprinkled throughout as if stars had fallen into her hair; her earrings sparkling all the way to the back of the room, and a smile that lit up the whole auditorium.

I begged my mind to hang onto that vision. That was the mom we were so proud of!

But as she started to walk down the stairs onto the stage to make her presentation... my heart sank.

I could see the moment she took her first step that she was drunk. It was that same familiar stumble I'd now witnessed a hundred times. With each step she took, I slumped deeper into my seat. I was sure my whole family was doing the same wherever they were sitting. I wanted to run out, but I didn't want to create a scene. Maybe others hadn't noticed.

When she spoke into the mic, her speech was noticeably slurred. But mom had such a great sense of humor that somehow she made her impaired speech into a joke that was really funny and the whole auditorium laughed hysterically. It really <u>was</u> funny, and I have to give her credit for that, but to me, it was the most humiliating thing I had ever experienced. She continued to slur her speech and continued to cover it up, and it continued to be hysterically funny as if purposely scripted that way. She had the whole auditorium in stitches. It was like a scene in a movie. Everyone was bent forward in their seats grabbing their sides in hysterics.

Except me.

I was devastated.

Finally, I couldn't take anymore and ran out of the auditorium into the bathroom and slumped to the floor crying. I was followed by my best friend who scooped me into her arms, and I finally admitted everything to her. The whole story came spilling out. It was the first time I had ever spoken of it. After years of covering it up, the walls came crashing down. Our little secret was out in the open for the whole town to know, and I was shattered.

The next morning when mom came into the kitchen, my brothers and I didn't say a word. Normally we would be telling her how beautiful she was and how well she had done and how proud we were of her. But this year was different. After what seemed a long time, she broke the awkward silence by timidly asking how she had done. I still cry remembering how meekly she asked that question. It breaks my heart. All that extraordinary confidence reduced to this feeble question. I told her how I felt about her being drunk and what an embarrassment it was to all of us.

She became enraged and defensive, and we began the biggest argument of our lives. I had finally lost it. I ended up going into her bedroom and pulling out the booze bottles from her dresser drawer. I held them in front of her and clinked them together as I stood in her doorway so she could not lie about it anymore. She chased me, yelling, and kicked me out of the house. As I ran outside, I threw the bottles on the driveway, and glass burst everywhere as the strong smell of bourbon slowly seeped into the pavement.

I left.

I went to my girlfriend's house. My dad and brothers visited me every night and tried to get me to come home, but I refused to return until mom got help.

Many weeks later, mom willingly went to Hazelden for rehab, and I returned home. I remember one day I received a call from Hazelden, "HowDEE Margo! This is Minnie Pearl. I just love your Mama! I love her so much it hurts!" And she laughed and laughed! I could hear mom laughing in the background. Minnie was mom's roommate, and I could tell they were having a blast! Minnie Pearl was the famous country comedian who always wore a hat with the price tag hanging from it. My mother also wore hats so I could see the two of them having the time of their lives. She promised to come and visit me, but she never did.

On the day mom was coming home, I made her a terrycloth robe, baked her a chocolate cake, and painted a bright 'Welcome Home Mom' banner and hung it over the doorway. We had a happy homecoming party for her. It was a great celebration! It meant the world to me that in front of the whole family, she apologized to me. She thanked me for finally forcing her to go to rehab. She told us stories of Hazelden and said she never felt better in her life. She looked radiant again, like our shining star.

Eventually, as with many addicts, she fell off the wagon. It was devastating for all of us, and mom's and my catfights returned and remained for the rest of her life. The moans rippled through our house regularly, "There they go again." When mom relapsed, I was her adversary, and our fireworks would erupt like a science project. I was still the whistle-blower, and she remembered that every time she drank.

She would fall off the wagon, go back into rehab, and fall off again. The disease had her firmly in its grip, and her drinking got progressively worse. It was sad to see such a beautiful woman, and wonderful mom, and community leader, and friend to so many disappear down this destructive path.

When I was in my mid 20's, I was teaching TM in Manitowoc Wisconsin. My parents were living in Pueblo West Colorado, and our family planned a reunion in Eau Claire around my birthday. My mom and dad had always traveled together, but for some reason that year my mom came to see me by herself, ahead of my dad's arrival.

It was about a week before the reunion. She flew into Manitowoc at a busy time for me. I was hosting a series of events at the TM Center. Leaders in every field including Chief of Police, Head of the AMA, School Superintendent, and others, came to the center to talk about problems in their respective civic departments and organizations. I would finish the talk with evidence-based solutions that explained how TM could address their workplace issues.

I was living behind the TM center in the same building. The center was a large sunny space in front of my apartment, big enough to hold 50 chairs. My apartment had two bedrooms and was roomy enough to house both of us when my mother came to visit.

However, my mother's visit soon turned tumultuous. She was so out of control with her drinking that I couldn't handle her. It got so bad, and I was so busy every night with a new speaker coming in, that I could barely keep it all together. I was beside myself. After three days of this impossible situation, I walked outside into my driveway and prayed, pleading with God for an answer.

After some time, I realized I had to ask my mother to leave my house. I couldn't believe it. I was kicking my mother out of my house! It was so difficult to do emotionally, but even more difficult getting her physically packed up and into the car.

I had a lecture in Steven's Point that evening, so I planned to take her to the bus station and get her on a bus to see my brother. I took her to the bus station, but there were no seats left. I looked at my watch, and there was just enough time to drive her there myself and still get over to Steven's Point to give the lecture on time. So that's exactly what I did.

I jumped back in the car and headed north. After we had gotten onto the highway, the first words out of her mouth were,"Mag, I never meant to hurt you."

She started recalling all the times she had insulted me, embarrassed me and flat-out lied to me. She told me how much she loved me and how she never wanted to hurt me. She told me she had a big sorrow deep in her heart for what she couldn't be to me. She just wanted to be a loving mother and share the normal emotions that she was supposed to share with her only daughter. But she was too caught up in her inner struggle. She couldn't be what she desperately wanted to be to me, and so she lashed out at me instead. Every time she did, she was aware of it, and it made her feel worse; her depression spiraled deeper, and she lashed out even more. It was a vicious cycle, and I was her target.

She apologized for all of it. Every single thing. I was astonished. She owned up to every deed she ever did and came clean. Her love rushed into my heart like a river breaking through a dam. For the first time in my life, I felt freely loved by my mother. I was her daughter, and she felt she'd let her little girl down. She wanted nothing more than to be a good mother to me but she couldn't do it. So she humiliated me instead. She hurt me every time her inner demon got the best of her, and that is why it was always so unexpected and made all the worse because it was in front of other people.

She told me she was actually lashing out at herself. It was self-anger directed at me. As she recalled specific events in vivid detail, we both cried as we relived the pain. We cried over the fights we'd had, and all the times she had embarrassed me. She admitted everything she had done and begged for my forgiveness, which I freely gave. She went on and on about how sorry she was for everything and how much she loved me—something I had never doubted.

I told her that I never doubted her love even in our darkest moments. But it was liberating and healing to hear her express it. Finally, after rehashing miserable events, we started laughing hysterically. And then we cried again. And then we laughed again. We were like two crazy girls laughing and crying, and laughing and crying. This went on for the entire 45 minutes of our drive.

Once we arrived, I checked her into a hotel. I placed her suitcase on the luggage rack, and she sat down on the bed. I kissed her on the cheek, said goodbye and turned to leave. As I walked out, I looked back at her sitting on her bed, her back to the door, her head straight ahead, staring. I took a long loving look at her, and for the first time in my life, I loved her without any burdens. "I love you, Mom." Then I turned and left to get to my lecture on time. It was the lightest I had felt in years.

Five days later I was on my way to Eau Claire to meet my family. It was the night before our family reunion. I was staying at my best friend's house when I got a call from my brother Mark.

"Margo, how are you doing?" His voice was noticeably frail.

"Fine Mark! How are you?"

"Oh my God, you haven't heard."

"Heard what?"

"Mom died last night."

"Mom……..di…??" I couldn't speak.

OH.
MY.
GOD.

My mother.
Whom I had just seen.
With whom I finally got everything right.
My adorned beauty queen mother
my hero
my nucleus
……was gone.

All that radiance, that graciousness, that style, the talent,
the fun—POOF! Gone. Just like that.

My world stood still as I grieved the thought of never
seeing her again. I cried unbelievably hard for about 20
minutes—and then I stopped.

And I have never cried for her since.

Because. I realized at that moment…that <u>most of the pain
in death is regret.</u> Regret that you can't go back to that
person to resolve anything or tell them you love them or
say those things you wish you had said. It's too late.
They're gone. You will never have that chance again. I did
not have that regret. My mom and I had resolved our entire
relationship the last time I was with her, not knowing that
would be the last time I would see her. For that reason I
was sad she was gone, but I did not suffer the intolerable
pain of regret. Not at all.

That realization has stayed with me my whole life. From
that moment on, I have done whatever it takes to resolve

everything in every relationship, so there is no regret if that person were to die.

Living with regret is the hardest part of death. It's the thing you could have done but didn't do; it's the thing that will eat you up long after they're gone, and it's too late. Death itself can eventually be dealt with because of its finality. It is irrefutably fated for all of us. But resolving issues and telling someone how you feel about them is something over which you have complete control. And if you let the opportunity for resolution pass you by, it will haunt you and cause inconsolable regret.

If you're sitting by a fire and a spark flies and lands on your arm, if you flick it off immediately there's no harm. But if you wait, it will burn you. So resolve issues right away. Don't wait. Flick it off before it harms you. You'll feel 10 pounds lighter if you do; you'll feel 100 pounds heavier if you don't.

Our reunion turned out to be her funeral. At the funeral, I found out what had happened after I left my mom. She took a cab all the way across the state of Wisconsin to see my other brother in Rice Lake. Mark could not handle her either, so he called my father in Pueblo West and asked what he should do since she was here to attend the reunion. Dad was getting ready to leave to join us, but he said to put her on a plane and send her home.

Once home, she found my dad's car packed and ready to leave for Wisconsin. Assuming she was no longer invited to go to the family reunion, she grabbed her dog, "Mac," threw her suitcase in her car, and left saying, "I will be there one way or the other." Hours later, when my dad was ready to leave, he received a phone call from the police in Colorado Springs. They found her dead in her hotel room. She had taken the drug Antabuse which is used to treat alcoholics and started drinking, and the results were deadly.

Through conversations with her friends at her funeral, I heard details of her last few days. While visiting Mark, she drove to Eau Claire to see each one of her closest friends. She arrived in each of their driveways, honking her horn and each friend came out to see her. They chatted for a while and then she continued to the next friend's house. She was saying goodbye to every one of her friends. They didn't know that she had such a terminal intent. But her soul was on a clear path out of this world, and she was spending her remaining time with those people she loved most dearly.

She did make it to the reunion "one way or the other" just like she said she would. Sadly, it was the other way. The last time I saw my mother, I didn't know that we were taking our last ride. Those precious 45 minutes set the framework for all my future relationships.

It seemed my mother wanted me to experience what it meant to resolve an afflicted relationship and what the effect of doing so would have on my life. There would have been many deep regrets, but because of her great gift, there were none. The effect was enormous and life-changing. The result, to this day, is that I remember my mother with no regrets and with a clear heart. And I keep all my relationships with everyone resolved, whatever it takes.

I realize that all the pain she inflicted on me could have been debilitating throughout my life and could have created relational issues for me. But because our entire relationship was resolved, the pain melted away and left no scars. The damage was healed in the forgiving, and with the resolve went the stories. So she left me free from our entire karmic battle, leaving no battle scars in her wake.

I will never forget seeing her face as she lay in her casket at the funeral home. Her whitish-blonde hair, her royal blue silk blouse, but her beautiful face was wrought in anguish.

She looked physically beautiful to most, but to me, behind her smile was agony. I could see it. It saddened me to know she died that way. She could never overcome her addiction, and her deep inner suffering showed up in her face at death.

I have pondered her pain and where it came from. She had a husband who adored her, kids who looked up to her and loved her, and friends galore. It was something deeper than that. It had to be something she lived with all on her own, deep inside and unreachable by others.

I remember washing my car with my dad many years later. I asked him what he liked most about mom. He answered, "I loved everything about your mother." Then I asked him what he would change if he could change anything about his life. He answered, "I wouldn't change a thing."

We need to live like that. With no regrets. Where we wouldn't change a thing. Where everything is resolved with everyone.

Since mom's death, I have used death as an adviser. If this

were your last day with someone—and you knew it—look at all the things you simply would not care about, look at what interactions would matter to you, what would be important. If you knew they were going to die in the next minute, you would surely forgive them for everything, and you would beg their forgiveness in return. You would express your love. You would thank each other. You'd laugh and cry and set yourselves free like my mother and I did. You would swoon in this extraordinary emotion in your last moments together.

Here is my invitation to you: Live like that now! As if every moment with someone is your last. Let it all go. Love them, enjoy them, have compassion for them, try to understand them, tolerate your differences and forgive them. Resolve everything now and be at peace.

Then you will only feel the sadness of not seeing them again. But you won't experience the unbearable agony of irreversible regret. There is a big difference. I can assure you.

Nothing survives its purpose, and neither did my mother. Her time was up. She exploded like a star, lit up our world, and then she was gone. Too soon.

A Supernova.
A starburst of color spanning the night sky.
Sprinkling blue glitter stars

and sparkling bright lights.

Absolute brilliance against a dark backdrop.

My Mother.
May she reach into your darkness and shine some light.

JOURNEY TO THE OTHER SIDE

Man, can war ever screw you up!

When my brother Mike came home from Vietnam, he was still the fun-loving life of the party. He was the same wonderful, generous and big-hearted person he had been when he left for war. But it was obvious to his friends and me that something deep inside him had changed, and for all the remaining years of his life, I tried to figure out what had happened. I watched war movies; I read articles, I spoke with other Vietnam vets. But it wasn't until I watched "Letters Home from Vietnam" that I understood what happens when an enthusiastic 18-year-old boy is sent to war to kill. The wide-eyed enthusiast quickly faces a horrifying reality that few of us will ever understand…the reality of war. The enthusiasm quickly breaks down to sheer terror and eventually turns into a hardened, callous resolve to carry out orders to kill.

I started to grasp the transformation that Mike's young heart had to endure. His heart erected a fortress around itself to survive. This fortress protected not only his heart but also his psyche, his conscience and his future in this world. Mike told me that he could spot a Vietnam vet a mile away by looking into his eyes. He could see the vacuous pit inside the soul of a fellow vet.

No wonder Mike drank. He never spoke of Vietnam except to tell me how his best buddy was killed right next to him. Mike told me that he was tormented by the fact that his friend with a wife and two young children had been the one to die while he was allowed to live. That's the one thing I

103

know for sure haunted him because those are the only words he ever spoke to me about his experience in Vietnam.

And so, like many vets from any war, Mike became an alcoholic. At first, his drinking was confined to evenings and weekends. It did not affect his effectiveness as a professional photographer and videographer.

He worked most of his life in the glamorous film world and lived large. He lived in LA and traveled the country mainly shooting infomercials. In his career, he came across many interesting people. Some major and minor celebrities, including Morgan Fairchild, Cheryl Tiegs, and Deepak Chopra. For many years, while in Denver, he shot photos of all the rock groups that played the Denver Coliseum. He has boxes and boxes of photos of Neil Young, Kiss, Fleetwood Mac with Stevie Nicks, The Eagles, U2, Jethro Tull, Uriah Heep, Ted Nugent, Leon Russell, Kansas, Grand Funk and the list goes on and on. Having a backstage pass gained him access to these groups, and his stories kept us ever entertained. Behind the lens, Mike was in his element!

Then he gave all that up to sail to the Virgin Islands and set up his home on his boat. After two hurricanes had blown him out of there, he landed at the docks of Marina del Rey California where his work dwindled and his happy hours increased. One fateful day Mike's boat sank and shortly after a heart attack sunk him. His death shot a hole in my heart that has never healed.

His death made me question everything I thought I knew about life and about what happens after we die. His is the death that shattered my windshield and smashed my paradigm to smithereens. I believed in reincarnation—that we would all see one another again in the afterlife, in another life. But Mike's death was so devastating to me that it made me question whether I actually <u>would</u> see him again, because…WHAT IF I DIDN'T? What if everything I believed in was wrong? That thought was so overwhelming to me that it made me question everything I knew to be true. And suddenly I wasn't sure of anything anymore. The possibility that I may never see Mike again—something I had never considered—was not something I could easily live with.

It made me realize how strange death is. Suddenly your loved one just disappears. Poof. Gone. You can't see them anymore. You can't feel them. Can't touch them. Can't talk to them. They're simply gone, and it's incomprehensible where they went. They just disappear.

At his funeral I found myself speaking these words:

"It's a difficult time, isn't it? When someone dies, especially seemingly prematurely, it doesn't make sense to us, and we find ourselves searching our minds for answers. It seems he was taken from us too soon. But someone doesn't think that. Someone thought it was exactly the perfect time for him to go. And so we search our minds to have that make sense to us.

"I see us all staring off, not in a spacey way, but very intentionally as if we're looking for answers in the air, as we try to process his not being here. He used to be right here with us, right before our eyes, could see him, feel him, talk to him, and now he's not here. And now we have to find a way to deal with that, to make sense of it. So we stare deeply and let the memories flood in so we can process his not being here…and by doing that we metabolize him into our being. And as we process more and more, we're absorbing him more and more into our heart, and the pain becomes less and less as we feel his presence within us. We absorb him into us, and then we feel the joy of him in our heart, and that's the value of memory. It lives on. That is our connection to eternity. That is our connection with the Divine. So this grieving and remembering is an important and natural process to go through so that we can all move on in joy without leaving each other behind. So although it doesn't make sense to us right now that he has been taken from us, it does make sense in the bigger picture. And what we have to do is: expand our heart and awareness to encompass that reality, and when we finally expand enough, it will make sense, and we will find peace. And that's the glory of life…expansion through the human experience to the realization of the divine. That's the purpose of any experience we don't understand. We have to expand to encompass it; we have to expand the limitations of our mind and embrace a greater understanding. And that's how we grow. My hope for all of us is that we find that peace sooner rather than later."

I searched for higher wisdom and found comfort in the words of Maharishi Mahesh Yogi:

When someone dies, it is because, at that point, their karma has become insurmountable in the present body. It is not possible to understand why death had to come when it did, and there is no point in assuming responsibility and guilt. The course of action is unfathomable.

Unfathomable. I was somehow comforted by that.

I was also comforted by something he had said about grieving. He said that when someone dies, it is natural to grieve; it allows the soul to know that they were deeply loved. But it is also natural that the grieving taper off, so the soul knows they are not a drag on our life.

I love that! It's important to realize that for the sake of the deceased as well as ourselves we need to grieve but then let them go so we don't hold them back. I was definitely in the phase of letting Mike know that he was deeply loved! I was grieving and not at all ready to let him go.

Conversations at his funeral were astonishing. An incredible assortment of people came to pay their respects—one hundred or more lined up to tell me Mike was their best friend. Among them a beautiful, wealthy woman in her 50s, a Hispanic man who owned a taco stand, all the guys on the dock, and his infomercial buddies. A homeless man in a wheelchair rolled up to me and said, "I'm homeless. Mike would always bring me shoes, blankets, food, and water. One night I was freezing on the street, and he lay next to me for body heat and saved my life. I would have died that night." He started to cry. This story was particularly poignant to hear. Mike told us how they would never leave a soldier behind on the battlefield. Now I saw that he didn't leave anyone behind on the battlefield at home either. He would see a vet on the street with a sign and always give them money even though he barely had enough to keep himself alive. It was powerful to meet this homeless vet. His story came to me in an unsolicited way and showed me Mike's compassion for everyone. If you are a friend or relative, you expect some amount of help or concern, but in Mike's case, he consistently offered the same humanity to complete strangers.

Through the course of this emotional evening, I found out that Mike was everyone's best friend. This is a legacy that few of us will leave behind. I heard stories from all walks of life all night long, and all held the common thread that Mike was their best friend.

Well, he was also mine.

Every day through a framed photo on my dresser, I remember my brother, my dearest friend, who had this seemingly effortless ability to make others feel extraordinarily special. His life was more a celebration than anything else, uplifting everyone around him.

As for my memories, there are too many to recount. He was my older brother, my protector, the one I always turned to if I needed anything. He had a great big perspective on life which always translated into humor. In fact, he would be interested to read this book! If God told Mike and me to choose one friend to go with us through this lifetime, we would have chosen each other. How fortunate he was and I am to be able to say this about all my brothers. We would have handpicked one another as best friends. Because we are.

My brother Mark tells a story of Mike:

"When I think of Mike, I feel he was blessed with a charisma that just attracted people. When we were kids, he always let his little bros tag along. He was such a considerate older brother. He had a sense of humor that we could really appreciate.

"Two stories that come to mind took place at the lake when he was married. He was with his wife, Yvonne. They were out in the boat, and Mike was trying to teach her how to drive. He thought that this was an important skill she should learn since they often went boating. But she was having none of it. She made it clear to him that she was not ever going to learn to drive the boat. So once the boat got up to speed and planed off, Mike jumped out!! She was left in the boat going full speed ahead, leaving her no choice but to drive it! Learn she did. Classic Mike.

"We took Yvonne for a boat ride in our smaller boat. We

drove it down the channel to the dam on Eau Claire Lake.
When the boat got close to the dam, Mike unplugged the
gas line and, of course, the boat stalled right in front of it.

"Yvonne didn't know what he had done. So Mike pulled on
the rope to start the motor, and of course, it wouldn't start,
and Yvonne was freaking out. He pulled harder and harder,
and the boat was getting closer and closer to the spillway,
and it still wouldn't start. When she started to cry, he
hooked the gas line back up and drove the boat away."

My brothers all thought that was a genius prank, but I hated
it for Yvonne!

Marty has a funny story about Mike:

"In 1972 I was living in Pueblo West, CO with my family.
It was about a half hour from Pueblo, and about 45 minutes
from the high school I was attending. I needed a car, which
my dad had bought for me so I wouldn't be so isolated and
could get to school and back.

"Mike was working and became a bit of a wheeler-dealer
for a while. He had met someone that liked to trade stuff.
Apparently, this guy had a couple of items that Mike was
interested in so Mike started collecting items he was
willing to trade for the items he wanted to get. And then the
deal went down.

"I had gone somewhere with my friends and got home in
the early afternoon. I walked in the front door of our
house—it was a three-story duplex. My apartment was
downstairs. If you turned to the left, you were in the living
room of my parent's part of the duplex. I entered and
turned left to go in the living room of my parents and on
the living room floor sat two reel-to-reel tape decks, one
Akai and one Teac.

"Mike was standing there with a big shit-eating grin and said, "What do you think?" I went over to where they were, and we started checking out the decks. They were nice! Later, we brought the tape decks downstairs in my apartment. We spent hours and hours recording our favorite music on these awesome reel-to-reel tape decks.

"After we played with them for a while, talked about how cool they were and about all the things we wanted to record on them, I asked Mike if he had seen my car. When I came home, I noticed it wasn't in the parking area in front of the house. Mike, with a sheepish look, said "I traded it. It was part of the trade that got us these cool tape decks."

"Whaaat?" I asked Mike how cool dad was going to think these tape decks are when he finds out that he traded them for the car he bought for me to get to school and back. Mike brushed it off, we talked about the decks some more, and then he was gone, off to work on some other deals.

"Mike left me sitting there with a cool tape deck and a harried mind. What the hell am I going to tell dad when he asks where my car is? Or when I have to ask to borrow his car to go to school? He buys me a car, so I can get to school, visit friends, and not feel so isolated being way out here in the prairie of Pueblo West. Mike trades it for a couple of tape decks. Classic.

"So, after spending the afternoon stressing the arrival of my dad—he's home. The time has arrived. Judgment day is here. It's time for the fan to start collecting what's going to be flying. Now, my dad was the greatest. A sweet, gentle, quiet, loving father who just wanted the best for his kids and always did the best he could to provide anything we wanted. But, he was human.

"And I was a teenager.

110

"At this period my dad and I weren't exactly seeing eye-to-eye. I wanted to have fun and have everything given to me on a golden spoon—my dad just wanted some reason to give it to me or, better yet, for me to earn it. To be a good son, to progress and become productive and to follow the rules of the household.

"Trading away a car he bought for me wasn't part of the plan as he saw it. Luckily, I don't remember much of what was said that night—but I have always felt bad for my dad. He was upset, as well he should be, and I heard about it that night. I'm not sure what, if anything, was said between my dad and Mike but hopefully Mike got a little of that riot act. It was his deal. I was just the kid with the car stuck in the middle. But, anger and animosity weren't qualities exercised by our parents, so the incident soon became the "remember that trade" story that gave us, at first, reserved chuckles and later, hearty laughter.

"Mike. He would do more deals. He would record more music, and he would continue to charm the world as he passed through it. He was a special guy. It was his charm and personality that made the deal, and it was these same traits that got him through any repercussions from the deal. He was excited about the trade he had made, and that excitement filled the room. It was the power of his personality and his sense of fun and adventure that made me forget about what was sacrificed. Instead, I took in the moment and basked in the possibilities for the sonic pleasure that sat at our feet. Possibilities. That's what he made happen. It was a part of who he was, and it was the reason people were drawn to him. He made life big. Little mistakes were forgotten because life's proportions were so much bigger when you were with Mike. He made life fun, and he made this deal fun and, even though I sometimes wonder—what the hell were you thinking—I laugh, and I remember.

"We had fun. We paid a price. But we got our money's worth because life had just gotten bigger. The possibilities of life had once again been explored and another moment of enjoyment and adventure had been experienced. Just another "moment" in being a part of Mike's world."

Some of my best memories of Mike were when he would take me out on his boat on a little lake in Fairfield, Iowa. It was called Walton Lake, and he rented a house there for years. We'd float around for hours, talking about life, what we had both been doing, what we were going through and it was lovely. We enjoyed our long talks. I had traveled around the world teaching TM, and he traveled around the U.S. shooting infomercials that touted the latest diet fads, wrinkle creams and before and after acne pictures. He told me that if he saw one more thigh with cellulite, he would scream.

Over the years Mike and I shared many mutual friends. When I was living in Fairfield and still married, our best friends were Andy and Betty Bargerstock. Betty was born in Asheville NC and wanted to move back to her home state to live, either in Asheville or the mountains of Blowing Rock. She and Andy wanted my (then) husband, Scott, and me to move with them. So one winter day Betty and I set out in a white-out snow storm on an exploratory trip to look into the possibility of all of us moving to North Carolina. A workable plan emerged for her family, but my path was diverted by divorce, my father's death and a new relationship which took me to Los Angeles.

My new boyfriend was a director of photography in the film industry. A whole new world emerged for me including buying an option on a film I started to produce. Despite this promising new life in California, I soon made a visit to Andy and Betty who had settled in Blowing Rock. After visiting for a week, I was utterly enthralled by the beauty of the mountains and the quality of life in this wonderful mountain town. I dropped my film, ended my relationship, sent for my belongings and never left North Carolina.

When spring rolled around, Andy called me to come over the following Friday to celebrate their daughter Caroline's graduation from high school. Betty was out of town, so Andy was putting on a graduation party for her. Caroline is like my daughter. I couldn't believe, though, that Andy would undertake such an event without Betty (or me!), so I didn't believe it was happening. It just didn't make any sense! So I didn't take it seriously and forgot about it.

The night of the so-called "party," however, I overheard my boyfriend Randy on the phone with Andy. He said quietly, but just loud enough so I could hear, "This is going to blow Caroline's mind!" That obviously caught my attention! I was shocked to hear something was actually happening. So with great curiosity, I popped into gear, got ready for the party and off we went.

When we arrived, much to my surprise, many of my good friends were there readying to film Caroline's surprise—whatever that was to be! I got there just in time to join in and felt so happy that I came!

The plan was to surprise her with a gift of a Chihuahua dog, a replica of the trademark Taco Bell dog that she loved from the TV commercials. That surprised me. Knowing Caroline as I did, I was sure she would have chosen a more exotic breed for herself. But hey! If that's what she wanted, then I was on board.

A large box was set up in the driveway. Andy showed us

113

the dog and put it in the box. Since I showed up, I was chosen along with Randy to go upstairs and blindfold Caroline and escort her downstairs. Andy encouraged us to bring her down quickly before the dog got excited inside the box. Keeping the dog quiet and perfect timing were the essential ingredients for this to work.

So we quickly and dutifully did our part. As we started down the steps with Caroline blindfolded, Caroline began giggling. She was so excited and truly didn't know what to expect. The anticipation in everyone present was palpable.

Meanwhile, the guests had finished the final preparations downstairs. The air both upstairs and down was buzzing with anticipation. It was fun but also a little nerve-racking because of the unpredictability of the dog.

When we reached the bottom of the stairs, we walked outside through the front door and guided her to the box. Removing her blindfold, Andy said, "Caroline in honor of your accomplishments this senior year, we arranged for this special gift for you inside the box. Please open it and see what it is." The camera was poised, and videotape was rolling from behind the box, towards Caroline, Randy and me.

As she bent over the box, I encouraged her to hurry as I was nervous the dog would start barking. She removed the lid to the box and took off the first layer of blankets. Then she removed the next layer of blankets, and then the next layer, and then….out of the box….popped ……my brother!!!!

"Oh my God!" I screamed!! And kept backing up, hands over my mouth, half crying, half laughing, and totally mind blown. Everyone laughed and cheered, and I was blown away! Caroline and everyone there including Randy was in on the surprise. My friends had all pitched in to buy Mike an airline ticket from LA to come and surprise me on my birthday. And they had planned this for six months! It was just after my birthday, and it was Caroline's graduation so it was a perfect set-up and one I would never suspect. It's unbelievable that not one of them breathed a word during all those months. The dog was borrowed from a neighbor who stood with Mike around the corner of the house. When Randy and I went inside to fetch Caroline, the dog was removed from the box, then Mike jumped inside, and they covered him with blankets.

I have it on video since it was ME they were videotaping! I was out of my mind with joy. Ecstatic. I finally stopped backing up and ran toward Mike and jumped into his great big hug. I was insanely happy to see him! That was one of the happiest moments in my life!

Mike always surprised me like that, but this one took the cake. I hadn't seen him for a long time. When I was in Egypt teaching TM many years before this, my birthday came along, and I said to my husband, "You know....Mike COULD show up here today." He had such a hankering for fun. He was always looking for the thoughtful thing to do to surprise you and make you happy. He took such delight in bringing joy to others. He was so joyful himself, and so much fun to be around. But this one BLEW MY MIND! And my heart! Totally.

This was the Mike we all knew and loved. His bigger than life personality made his absence after his death all the more difficult. The hole in my heart was huge.

No longer in his body and without his body to confine it, his spirit was revealed. All the crevices you couldn't see before were now exposed, and every single thing that he meant to me and everyone else became clear. There are veils that hide things in the physical world that are no longer there when the body is gone. That's why it's natural that when someone dies, you realize how MUCH he or she meant to you. You couldn't know it as clearly when the veils were up.

Now that the facades were all gone, I could see his great soul clearly. His power was magnified in his death.

To see him in this new light was a majestic sight. He was a leader. His friends called him Senator. He attracted friends with uncommon grace and was a friend to all. A best friend. He didn't judge people; he didn't gossip; he was friendly to strangers and kind to everyone. He touched so many lives. A friend emailed me and said, "He was such a sweet soul with a big heart—perhaps one so big that its eventual breakage was inevitable. Very many people count themselves as better for having known him and I among them. He will be missed."

After Mike's memorial service, I was back in the hotel room with Betty. I asked her, "Should I have offered for Mike to come and live with me or offered some help in case he wanted to quit drinking?" She answered an emphatic, "NO!"

I asked her why. She explained to me that Mike was living with her family in Fairfield when he took the advanced TM Sidhi Course. She said he became such a bright light. He looked fantastic! He was always handsome and charismatic, but now even more so with bright light shining through those beautiful blue eyes. He was doing so well. He was having fun, working hard and feeling great. He had quit drinking and was on top of his game.

Then one night Mike came home very late and drunk. Betty, shocked, got out of bed and went into the kitchen and asked him what happened? Mike looked her straight in the eyes and said, "Betty, I want to drink, and I'm going to drink!"

I was stunned to hear that story. I had to take that deep inside and figure out what that meant in the bigger picture. I remembered a quote that I had kept on my desk for years that said if you resist a desire, it drives the desire deeper into your subconscious. It's a tantric principle to go straight into your desires and not avoid or deny them.

I realized that we were all born with an alcoholic gene in our family. I was supposed to overcome it and did right out of college. One day I realized that I was walking down the same path as my alcoholic mother and through a series of events I quit cold turkey and never drank again.

Mike, on the other hand, wasn't supposed to overcome it. He chose to go right down the middle of it—that night in Betty's kitchen. In doing so, he became a great alcoholic. What I mean by that is, he wasn't one of those mean beat-up-your-kids-falling-down drunks. He was quite the opposite. He loved people, loved his friends, was generous and kind-hearted, thoughtful, fun and funny. He made people happy and was loving and considerate. He had many friends because he was such a true friend and genuine person. He reached out to people he would have never met if he didn't drink.

He affected people so deeply that, to this day, his friends call me on his birthday and his death day when they are out celebrating with his ashes. They had put his ashes in a beer bottle and poured part of them in the ocean between a circle of sailboats at their favorite Catalina Island. The other part stayed in the bottle that has now grown into a shrine by everyone attaching something to the bottle everywhere they go. They always have him with them.

117

Mike lived his life so well. He lived alcoholism so well. And even though it destroyed his body, in the end, I know the alcoholic gene is burned out of him. He no longer has any alcoholism in his being or his karma. He went straight through the middle of it, enjoyed it, wrestled with it, but in the end burned it right out of existence.

He may not have struggled with it. It just became a part of him. He didn't make any bones about it, no complaints, no trying to change, just enjoyed it and enjoyed his life despite it. That's why I say he was good at it. He didn't harm anyone and in fact, uplifted everyone. It was fun to be around him whether he was drinking or not. It made no difference.

As in the deaths of other loved ones, I needed to see his face in death. When I did, I saw that his transition happened in an instant. I saw it in his expression. He was taken by surprise and was fascinated. It was a surprise journey just like everything else in his life. He was always surprising others, so it seems fitting the ultimate surprise was on him!

When he was alive, he was fascinated with every little thing. He used to come up to me, wide-eyed, with something in his hands and say, "Wow. Look at this!" And it was some little gadget he had come across that caught his attention and triggered his imagination. He would show me how it worked and thoroughly enjoyed whatever it was. Over and over again, another little phenomenon caught his attention. In his death, it was the same experience, except this time the phenomena took him off guard into a surprise adventure he wasn't prepared for. Nonetheless, by his expression, it looked like he was anticipating a good time!

I knew God would not have him suffer. He didn't deserve that kind of death. When I stood with him in the viewing room, I spontaneously started singing the puja. It didn't even sound like my voice. It had a celestial quality to it. He lay there bathed in pure light; out of his body, in front of and a little above me. I was in sheer appreciation as I reflected on his life and what it meant and how he touched so many people so deeply. His was a life well lived. As I was leaving the viewing room, I turned to Mike, hands together in the "Namaste" position, and said, "Well done!" I was honored to witness such greatness of being.

I seldom remember my dreams, but I had many dreams of Mike after he died. In every one of them, he came to me to tell me he had not died.

After I had returned from his memorial service in LA, I attended a real estate developer's party in Charlotte on Friday night. While there I met two college students from Boone, Peter, and Brian. We had dinner and then I went back to my room and fell asleep.

In the early morning, before I awoke, I had a dream that Peter and Brian had come to my room to pick me up to return to Boone. Suddenly, while standing in the door of my hotel room, as I was putting my bags in the hallway, Mike came sweeping through the door! I jumped, startled, shocked. I exclaimed," Oh my God! Mike! What are you doing here?" And he grinned and put his fingers up to his mouth, as if to mimic biting his nails and said, "I didn't die." I told him, "But Mike we just had a memorial service for you in LA!" And he said, "Yeah but I'm not dead. I didn't die." I was SO freaked out and asked him where he had been, and he said: "Cleveland" (remember it was a dream! You know how dreams go).

Later a friend said that Cleveland was probably true...he was in "Cleve land."

My younger brother commented that "Cleveland is kind of like dying!"

Anyway, the dream was real…Mike was there in spirit as real as in person. I have heard of many experiences of souls contacting their loved ones after they die. They often come in dreams. So when I call this a "real" dream what I mean is that it was a real visit from my brother on what some would call the astral level. It was not your typical distorted dream but one that was lucid and experienced exactly as you would have experienced that person on the physical earthly plane. Although it is not physical, it is nevertheless real.

During that week Mike came to me many times in dreams, and they had similar themes. In one dream, wherever I went Mike was there right next to me, arms folded firmly across his chest as if to say, "See, I'm here." If I were talking to a friend, he would sit right next to me, really close and I could see him but they couldn't. My friend Jessica walked into a restaurant where I was eating, and Mike was sitting right next to Jessica, and she talked to me but didn't see him. Everywhere I went Mike was there, but no one could see him but me. He was always standing right next to me, purposely, as if to say, "Here I am!" He was everywhere, all the time, right next to me, pressing his body close to mine so people would see him as they looked at me.

One day I was in my shower crying SO hard I could hardly stand up. Just as I was finishing, the middle light on my mirror started to flicker. That light had been dead for years. It was an electrical problem, so changing the bulb didn't help. So when the light started to flicker, I KNEW it was Mike. He was a lighting expert in the film industry. I knew he was manipulating something familiar to him to get my attention. Mike could be very intense when he wanted something, so he used this obvious means to get my attention.

When the light began to flicker, I started talking to him as if he were in the room. I was jabbering away and finally, just to make sure, I said to him, "Okay Mike, help me out here. I'm talking to a light bulb thinking it's my brother! So if it's really you, stop for a minute and then blink the light three times." So the light stopped for a minute. But it didn't come back on again. I waited for a little while, and it didn't flicker. My heart sank. I was sure it had been him. I opened the door to leave the bathroom and suddenly—it <u>flickered three times!</u> I rushed back in and started talking to him again like a crazy person! I have no idea what I said. I just went on and on about everything I could think of. I was so excited! I even apologized to God for talking to a light bulb thinking it was my brother!

Finally, I had to leave, and I said." Mike, I have to go. I have an appointment. But stay right here…I'll be right back. Don't leave! I'll be back in one hour!" (AS IF he was confined to the light bulb in my bathroom!!) I laughed out loud!

The night after the light bulb incident I got a call from Steve, Mike's friend in whose house Mike was living when he died. Steve reported having weird dreams of Mike every single night since he died. I told him I was too! So we compared notes…and suddenly we both realized…

Mike did not know he was dead.

He had slipped out of his body so fast and so effortlessly that he did not realize that he wasn't in it anymore. From his perspective, he was simply embarking on yet another grand adventure.

I believe that in an experience of sudden, unexpected death, slipping out of one's body may not be immediately obvious to the departing soul. It happens as effortlessly as shrugging off a coat so it wouldn't necessarily seem very different. In Mike's case, there had been no prior mental preparations for death, as there would be in the case of prolonged illness, so he could easily not have been aware that he had dropped his body. I remembered seeing the surprised look on his face. He was definitely on to the next adventure; he just didn't know the adventure had taken him out of his body.

I spoke to my friend Charlie that night who convinced me that I needed to help Mike understand that he had died. It was about two in the morning when I hung up the phone. I sat on the bed, drenched in tears and ready to help my brother with this truth. I said, "Mike you are here. But you are not in your body anymore. You left it at Steve's house. You dropped it just like you would let your coat drop to the floor. And that is why I am so sad because I can't see you anymore. I can't be with you. You are not on the physical plane anymore. You no longer have a body. In fact, we burned it, so it doesn't even exist on this earth anymore. It is now just ashes. THAT is why you see me crying so hard all the time because I can't be with you ever again on this earth. Your spirit is here, but your body is not. You are dead."

I could feel, as I was saying this to him, that it was making sense to him on the other side. I could sense that whatever his spirit guides had been telling him was starting to make sense. They had been trying to explain to him, but he had not been able or willing to understand. As I kept explaining the situation I could feel his dawning realization as he put the puzzle pieces together. After about half an hour, I stopped with the explanation and the tears and drifted off to sleep. I didn't dream of him that night or ever again. He was gone. He was dead, and now he knew it.

A couple of nights later, I had some friends over for a celebration of Mike's life. I had learned from my friend Tom Shirah's recent death that ten days after someone dies is the ideal time to celebrate because the departed soul has "processed" and can be more present with you.

I was very sad that evening. We had a wonderful dinner. I had Mike's pictures all around with flowers and candles, we watched a slideshow of his life with many of his own photographs, and then we said a prayer. At the end of the evening, I told my friend Debra about my experience with Mike—the dreams, his not knowing he was dead and his absence since the conversation explaining that he was. I asked her if there was anything she could do to check on him for me. Since Debra had training and a natural ability in this arena, she agreed to take a look. She told me to call her the next evening from my hotel in Charlotte on my way to Mike's funeral in Eau Claire.

When I called Debra back at the appointed time, she took me on the most extraordinary shamanic-like journey. She first led me through a series of breathing exercises which prepared me for this undertaking. With her instruction, I closed my eyes and envisioned a path, and she guided me along it.

I visualized a North Carolina mountain path that was cold and damp with leaves flattened into the dirt and trees towering above. I felt the path as I proceeded. I even bent down and touched the damp, hard earth beneath my feet. I walked along the path, vividly aware of my surroundings— the colors, the coolness of the earth, the sun sparkling through the trees. The path was beautiful and the smells sublime, like a forest filled with scents of pine and green leaves after a fresh rain.

At one point I came across steep stairs going down on

either side of the path. At that point, I had trouble continuing forward. I felt stuck. Nonetheless, Debra herself had moved further along the path. To catch up with her, I had to force myself to push away from the stairs and run.

I caught up with her, and we walked until we came to the edge of the woods. She asked me if I saw a meadow and yes, I did! There it was spread out before me, sprawling lush green grass sprinkled with wildflowers and rimmed with Mountain Laurel, some lovely purple butterfly bushes, and a slight floral scent. It was heavenly. She told me to look across the meadow, and I did.

"Is Mike there?" She asked.

"YES!"

He was! He was standing on the other side of the meadow just as clearly as anything in real life.

"He's been waiting for you. He wanted to say good-bye."

I burst into tears. He came over to me and hugged me with HIS hug. I could feel him with his beautiful arms around me JUST as in real life. We held each other and Debra told me to take as much time as I needed.

So I talked excitedly and told him everything I could think of to tell him. We laughed and talked and enjoyed, and I was so happy to be with him again. I was beside myself with relief to see him, and the sheer joy that filled my being was beyond anything I could imagine—just to be with him again! I will never, ever be able to explain the actual feeling of those endless moments we shared. Never. The world could have gone away. It could have ended, and I wouldn't have known or even cared. I would have stayed there <u>forever</u> if I hadn't heard Debra's voice gently pierce our euphoria.

"Now take his hand and walk him back across the meadow."

So I did.

"Do you see some stairs?"

"Yes."

"Walk up the stairs."

"Do you see the white light?"

"Yes."

"Walk towards the light."

I want to say this was surreal but it was real. We must have taken two steps, and she said,

"Now let go of his hand."

And I did. I couldn't believe I could do it. I did not want to let him go. But I did so without hesitation. It was the saddest thing I have ever done. I watched as he kept walking. He never looked back.

Debra asked me to turn around, to walk away from the light and to go back down the stairs, making sure the light was behind me. She said to walk back across the meadow and if I saw anyone else, not to mind, just to keep walking and to pay no attention to them. So I turned around, walked down the stairs, and back across the meadow. I walked the cold path past the downward stairs on both sides and back to the beginning of the path.

I hung up the phone, and I cried harder than I have ever cried in my life…deep into the night.

When I woke up in the morning, I was exhausted and

empty. I boarded a plane to Eau Claire for his memorial service. While on the plane, I thought back to the experience of the night before. I could see that in the meadow he realized that he was dead. And he was telling the people on the other side, "Yes, yes I know I'm dead, I'll be right with you, but I <u>have</u> to say goodbye to my sister." I appreciated the stubbornness and adamancy with which he did things in his life because that same quality allowed him to say goodbye to me now. I will never forget that extraordinary experience. I was actually <u>with</u> my brother on some plane.

Later that day I asked Debra what the stairs represented because I had such a hard time getting beyond them. She said it was the end of the subconscious mind. I found that very intriguing. Once I got past that point, I was on some "plane" that contained souls that were in some sort of holding pattern, for various reasons. In Mike's case, he was so full of life while he was alive and he left his body so quickly and unexpectedly, that he just didn't realize he had died. So he kept trying to tell me in any way he could, the light bulb, the dreams, that he was still alive. Until he finally realized, when I finally realized what was going on and told him.

That shamanic experience settled something in me. After that, something in my awareness shifted dramatically. I knew he had moved on.

I came to terms with that. I realized that Mike's life on earth was complete. He experienced all that he came here to experience. The timing of his death was perfect, and I knew that his death was also his new birth. It brought to mind a poem I read at his funeral by Bishop Charles Henry Brent:

A ship sails and I stand watching till she fades on the

horizon   And someone at my side says, "She is
gone." "Gone where?"
Gone from my sight, that is all;
She is just as large as when I saw her.
The diminished size and total loss of sight is in me, not
in her.
And just at the moment when someone at my side says,
"She is gone"
there are others who are watching her coming,
and other voices take up a glad shout,
"Here she comes!"
.....and that is dying.

Around the first anniversary of his death, I had another
dream. This was the first dream I'd had of Mike since his
realization that he had died. It was another real dream. I
call these real dreams because they really happen and are
tangible on some level. An authentic message is
communicated as in real life, and the effect on me is just as
real.

My dream took place in a theatrical playhouse where there
was a wide hallway and many doors that opened onto that
hallway. In the dream, I was in the hallway, and the doors
suddenly opened admitting a crowd of people. I saw Mike
come out the door and he was easy to see because he was
about a foot above everyone else. As he crossed the
hallway, I saw that he was about 30 years old and
uncontrollably handsome with that contagious smile. Our
eyes met and melted into each other at the recognition. We
hugged a great big Mike hug, and I could feel him again
just as if we were both in human bodies—just as we had
felt in the meadow. It was the same real hug.

Once again, I was so excited to see him that I talked a mile
a minute. I asked him what he's been doing since I last saw

him, and he told me stories that were odd dream-like stories that didn't make sense. Then I told him I wanted to see him again. I told him that I wanted to be with him again and asked when we would be together again. That is when the quality of the dream slowed down a bit and became seriously real. "It's not about when we will see each other again; it's so much more than that."

I was surprised at his response, so I asked," Like what?"

He said, "It's about what you do."

Then I woke up.

When I woke up, I had to go deep with that thought. I had to let my mind ponder "It's about what you do." I had to understand his message to me and what it meant exactly. Here is what I came to realize.

In every moment we are "doing" something. It is about what we "do" and how we are in each moment that is important. People are constantly passing through our moments. Some people pass through them more often and consistently than others, like a spouse, siblings or parents. But it's not about being with them. It's about what we do and how we are in our moments—with or without them in it. It's about us and how we are being, not who we are with. Who we are with comes and goes while we're doing what we do. It's about what we do.

That was slightly devastating to me. I wanted to hear from Mike that I would see him again.

I instantly saw my life like this: Our eyes are like projectors. We see out through them, and people and events come in front of us. Some people come in front of our projector more than others. Everyone comes and goes, events constantly change before our eyes, but we are quietly behind the scenes looking and experiencing through the projector, living our moments whether people are there in front of us or not. THAT is what we do. We live moments. We constantly choose to live them in a certain way, and how we choose to live them is what matters.

I reflected on Mike's life. What a great example he was of living his moments well no matter who he was with. He lived them to the fullest. It didn't matter if you were a beggar on the street or a movie star or his sister. He lived with fullness and love for all. Of course, this would be his message to me. This gift replaced, to some extent, the sadness I felt in realizing that it isn't important whether I'm with him again or not.

Instead, I was left with thoughts of how to live my moments and how to BE in my moments from Mike's example: Live well. Be kind. Let the smallest things in life fascinate you. Be grateful for and return the smallest kindness. Laugh a lot. Be sweet. Surprise people. Spread happiness. Be attentive to elders. Help the homeless. Be thoughtful. Live humbly. Leave no one behind. Be everyone's friend. Be grateful for every breath, and with every breath, serve your Master, be it God, or whatever you perceive that to be. Live your truth. ENJOY your life. Live it, guzzle it, chug it! Live everything fully. Have a good time! Be sensitive to others. Live with dignity no matter what your circumstance. Treat others with dignity no matter what theirs.

Live like this with whoever shares your moments with you. Do what you do and do it well. Live your moments with dignity and grace and live them beautifully and love-fully. How we live each moment is what matters.

However, I have to admit, even as I write this to you: What I wouldn't give to have ONE MORE MOMENT with my brother. I would give anything for it.

I would give it all up for just one moment with him.

But it's not about that.

THE MIRACLE PIE

"The Miracle Pie takes the cake!" said my friend.

I felt like I had known Tom for lifetimes when we met; old souls coming together for another rendezvous.

We met while in the Philippines on a huge TM teaching project. He was part of a men's organization that had devoted their lives to promoting world peace through the practice of TM in large groups.

It had been found through scientific research that when 1% of any given population practiced TM that crime rates dropped as well as sickness rates and accident rates. Because of the 1% effect, thousands of teachers of TM were called to the Philippines by Maharishi Mahesh Yogi on the one year anniversary of the assassination of Benigno Aquino, Jr. He was a former Filipino Senator and a longtime political opponent to then-dictator Ferdinand Marcos. Maharishi sought our presence there to prevent the expected riots and bloodshed in Manila.

Besides taking part in the activities of the TM organization, Tom was an accomplished musician and formed a band with five other men of equal talent. In their spare time, they traveled the country playing various venues. I thought I was their biggest fan until I saw they had young Filipino girls all over the country ogling over them. I saw an entire busload of schoolgirls singing along to the lyrics of their most popular song on the radio, "Mabuhay"! They all sang loudly with smiles on their faces and crushes in their hearts.

We taught TM to thousands of people in the Philippines and prevented the dreaded riots. In fact, when the day came, we watched the gathering from our hotel room windows, and it was like a party. In contrast to the anticipated bloodshed, everyone was having the time of their life.

Feeling successful, after eight months, we went home.

The next time I saw Tom was 20 years later when I moved to Blowing Rock. He was there with the same men's organization, doing the same thing: creating world peace. But this time from the Blue Ridge Mountains of North Carolina.

This time, we spent 10 years seeing each other whenever we could, over lunch or a cup of tea, him playing gigs in town, at parties when he could sneak away from the group. Tom came running whenever I needed help on my computer, had something go wrong at the house, needed a friend to do something with or a shoulder to cry on. We were best of friends.

At one point, he left his men's group and got together with a friend of mine named Ann. They soon moved in together, and naturally, I didn't see Tom as much as I had.

One day I ran into him as we passed each other on the road. We both rolled down our windows and talked from our cars. He complained of a terrible backache that wouldn't go away. I told him if he had a backache he needed to see my chiropractor friend, Tim Musick, who was a little over an hour away in Abingdon, VA.

So the next day I picked Tom up at his house and took him to see Tim. Tim worked on him for a long time, and the next day Tom felt a little better. But the day after that he felt bad again, so I took him back to Tim. Tim explained that after what he had done two days before, if Tom wasn't feeling better, then he needed to get an MRI. Something was seriously wrong. That news freaked Tom out.

I told Tom I thought he needed to get tested to see what was wrong. No matter what the result was, he didn't have to go the normal medical route if he didn't want to. We'd figure out something alternative, but it was important to know what he was dealing with.

He waited a long time. It was several months before he was up for finding out what was wrong with him. When he finally did the tests, he found out he had lung cancer. It was so advanced that the tumors were wrapped around his spine, and they couldn't operate.

He immediately started chemo and went downhill fast. We began a series of long talks from that moment on. In the middle of conversations about other things, he would suddenly start to cry and tell me how he wasn't ready to say good-bye to his friends and his life.

On the last day that I saw him still coherent, now in the hospital, I said to him, "Tom, you have so much light in you that nothing has changed. Your body is 90% gone, but you are still the same. Nothing's changed." His face was bright and shining.

A few days later, Ann called me early in the morning and said the hospital had called her to come in immediately, that he had gone into a coma. We held a vigil in the hospital that day. About seven of us sat with him non-stop all day long until they kicked us out. He remained in the coma.

The next morning I went to the hospital early because I knew this would be the last time I'd see him and I wanted to spend some quality time with him before everyone else started filing in. My boyfriend Ron had died a couple of weeks earlier, and his family was arriving today for his memorial service.

It was about 8 AM when I walked into the hospital room. Tom was lying in bed with just a sheet over him, all hooked up to IVs and breathing from a machine. I sat quietly for a while and then got up and walked over to him. I stood real close to him and said, "Tom, I am standing right next to you, looking into your face. You know how well we always communicate. I am looking into your eyes right now. I have to know….are you in there?" Immediately—he blinked his eyes! I got so excited I shrieked—out loud—and started to jump up and down, "Oh, my god! Oh my god! Tom!

It turns out that when he blinked, his eyes stayed open ever so slightly. Just a slit. When I looked at the slit in his eyes, I could see that he was smiling. They were filled with delight at my response to his communication with me.

Then I proceeded to talk to him for quite awhile. After some time I felt I needed to let him rest. From time to time I'd think of something else to tell him and then sit quietly again and then talk some more, then quiet. This continued for about two hours until the others started to arrive.

Just after noon, I received a call from Ron's sister that his family had arrived. So I quietly walked over to the other side of Tom's bed and looked straight into his eyes. I said everything I wanted to say to him. I thanked him for being such a great friend and for always being there for me; I expressed how I will miss him and how I will look for him again. I told him I loved him.

As I talked, I could see the slit fill with tears. I couldn't say another word after that. We shared a quiet, deep, emotional farewell.

He died five minutes after everyone left his room that night.

We held his memorial service at our good friend's Mac and Diane Gayden's house on his birthday five days later. Tom and Mac had played music together on many occasions and had become very good friends.

The service was one very moving event. I can't imagine a better tribute to a musician than this one done for Tom. When we got ready to start, I was expecting Diane to get up to the mic and lead the ceremonies. But she insisted I do it, stating that she was too shy and didn't have any idea what to say.

Neither did I, but spontaneously, and surprisingly, up I went. It was heartfelt; it was moving, it was a celebration fit for our beloved friend and talented musician.

Here is my recap of the day that I posted on Tom's website the next day:

Yesterday was one of the loveliest days in my memory. The setting was sublime and perfect for Tom's celebration. It was so appropriate to be at Mac and Diane Gayden's beautiful home where Tom played, and we enjoyed so much exceptional music over the years.

The day was glorious and sunny with a slight breeze, and, if you know Mac and Diane, you can imagine how beautiful their home and yard looked; the setting was truly "Gayden"! There were round tables outside with table cloths, flowers, and candelabras, and a table with pictures of Tom. In the corner facing the house, so guests faced the gorgeous view of the Blue Ridge Mountains, was the microphone and instruments for the musicians. Inside was beautifully and artfully Diane, and full of food!

People shared stories, musicians sang and played, the sun was shining, and the fall day was perfect. We were all in a sad and happy soup together, a floaty sublime feeling. It was soft and gentle but extra poignant because Tom was extra special. He had a rare bright light that we were fortunate to enjoy, and we will enjoy again, but meanwhile, we will deeply MISS.

Mac sang a rare rendition of "Everlasting Love"; Ken Laderoute played his guitar, and Amy sang "It Comes from Me" from a place I believe she's never come from before; Stella Vera Kilcher sang a beautiful song about coming from the Divine; and the Grammy goes to Steve Davidowski who played the saxophone as he slowly walked away from the party, down the hill, pausing here and there to let his music resound and softly echo through the valley. It was out of this world.

Tom's best friend Marty made a DVD in Tom's honor showing his life and music in many different settings which allowed us to celebrate him fully! There wasn't a dry eye in the room when the DVD finished with Tom himself singing "Happy Trails."

Another friend caught on film two pieces of exceptional footage: a triple rainbow the day we were holding the 13-hr vigil at Tom's bedside at the hospital; and four golden eagles circling over Heavenly Mountain directly above Tom and Ann's house the day he died. He was a film producer and masterfully combined the eagle's footage with the triple rainbow to create a stunning tribute. He hadn't even met Tom but understood the significance of what he saw and got it on record. So we played that DVD, and it was powerful.

We had a hard time leaving. Diane played a song that her daughter Oceana wrote for Tom, with these lyrics:

"I'm raining peaceful. I'm closed for the season, check back with me in the spring...when the sweetest air will sing to me, and the flowers bloom to remind you....I'm not afraid of the sky, I'm not afraid to go higher."

It was beautiful, and Tom got to hear it just hours before he left us.

Tom was honored.

Thanks to everyone who loved Tom, you were all there with us yesterday.

It was a beautiful mosaic of tales and tears and music, and we sent him off in—his style! Beautiful unrehearsed perfection!

After the funeral, we heard from a sage friend of ours that we should do the memorial ten days after the person has passed because their spirit is processed and will be more present. Since we had already held the Memorial Service, Ann decided to have a dinner party for 17 of us at her home on the 10th day.

On walking through her front door, I noticed the air was light, and Tom's presence was palpable. Everyone commented on it. There was a banquet table set for 12 in the dining room and a round table set for five in the kitchen.

We had a fun, wonderful evening telling "Tom stories" all night long in his honor. At the end of the meal, Ann brought out an apple pie, announcing that Debra had brought dessert for everyone. It was a pie that served six!

Upon realizing that this was our only dessert, Debra said under her breath, "I'm not having any." I said, "I'm not having any." Mac, who was sitting across from me, followed with "I'm not having any." We quickly realized that the people who would be enjoying the pie were those in the kitchen who didn't know how small the pie was!

Ann proceeded to place 17 plates in front of Debra and me, and we dove into the task of cutting and serving the pie. I handed the first plate to Mac who passed it toward the kitchen. Then the 2nd plate went toward the kitchen and the 3rd. Meanwhile, we were enthusiastically telling "Tom stories," and laughing and pausing to listen and serving pie, and telling another story and serving pie and laughing and serving pie.

Suddenly someone from the kitchen yelled, "We all got pie!" With that Debra and I looked around and realized that everyone at the banquet table also had pie. And there was one large piece left in the pie pan that we could cut in half…and then Debra and I would have pie…and therefore—we ALL had pie.

We were BLOWN AWAY! We were stunned. We looked at each other in utter disbelief! We were absolutely speechless! Then under our breath and in unison, we said, "Loaves and fishes." That small pie had just served 17 people!

Debra and I were out of our minds! I started to laugh, then Mac laughed, and then Debra. Just then someone asked me to tell a particular story about Tom. So I began the story. Only a few words into the story I interrupted myself by bursting out laughing, and said to everyone, "Do you realize we ALL got pie?" I dropped my head into my hands and laughed uncontrollably. It was incredible. I couldn't even fathom what just happened. I had tears streaming down my face.

Just then I looked up from my fit of laughter, and I saw, in my mind's eye, a vision of Tom above us with this "white stuff" in his hands that looked like clouds, but with a little more weight than clouds. He was throwing the stuff up in the air, tossing it, and picking up more and tossing it and smiling his big Tom smile, as if to say, "There's plenty! There's absolutely plenty! It's everywhere!" He was having so much fun, heaving this "stuff" into the air.

A few minutes later Cyndy walked from the kitchen over to where we were sitting and saw the size of the now empty pie plate and said, "Oh! It's a miracle pie!"

That night I was lying in bed, and I couldn't sleep, I couldn't stop laughing. I called Debra and left her a message on her voicemail. I said," Debra, I'm trying to see in my mind where the pie came from! Did we serve it all and it all came back? Did we serve one piece and the piece grew back? Did none of the pieces ever leave the pan at all until we were down to our last six pieces? WHERE DID IT COME FROM?" I could not stop laughing. I was mystified.

We had witnessed a miracle, and God, in his infinite wisdom, kept us busily telling stories while the miracle was taking place so we would not be in on the mystery until it was over. In my mind's eye, for the longest time, I tried to "see" where that pie came from. I've since given up. To quote a great musician, Adam Musick, in his song "Outside Figure": "….said I'd tell you, but there'd be no mystery."

Life is meant to remain a mystery. I am convinced of that. We'll never figure it out. We just get little glimpses here and there to help us along the way. But we will never figure it out.

This story has taken its rightful place in my life. From that moment on, I have never doubted that there is plenty. We will always have enough. We will always have what we need. There is an infinite resource in the universe. There is plenty for all of us.

I can still see Tom throwing the stuff into the air, tossing it around as if there was no need to hold any back. He would never run out; it would never run out. I will never run out, and we will never run out. I was in on a big secret; it cemented my faith in God.

Tom's miracle pie serves us all.

If I ever doubt, I remember the white stuff.

LIGHT IN THE TUNNEL

She was 91 in human years.

She was running around the rocks, having the most delightful time of her 13-year old dog life! She was willed to me when my friend Ron died, and his generous bequest turned out to be one of the great gifts of my life.

Casey was romping around like a teenager, so I assumed her tumor was not cancerous. I felt that except for the tumor, she was doing just fine.

We were at Table Rock which rims Linville Gorge in the mountains of western North Carolina. That area is renowned for its ley lines that run beneath the earth's surface. According to Page Bryant, in her book, *The Spiritual Reawakening of the Great Smoky Mountains,* Table Rock is a powerful planetary energy vortex. According to her, "A vortex is a mass of energy that moves in a rotary or whirling motion, causing a depression or vacuum at the center." She goes on to say that "These powerful eddies of pure earth power manifest as spiral-like coagulations of energy that are either electric, magnetic, or electromagnetic qualities of life force." So we decided to go and *feel* the power at Table Rock. The week before, for the same reason, we had hiked nearby Hawksbill, another dominant peak and power point with the ley lines going in the reverse direction, according to Page.

Once at Table Rock, my partner Steve and I were relaxing with Casey at the top of the mountain. We looked toward neighboring Hawksbill when suddenly, seemingly out of nowhere, rose a swirl of birds from the flatland below. First, we noticed a few and then hundreds and then maybe thousands came into view all flying in a slow rising spiral. It was awesome. It was a phenomenon. I caught it on camera and kept asking Steve if he saw it as my eyes were focused on the birds through the camera lens. He did, and we were both transfixed by the spectacle in the sky. This went on for about 15 minutes, birds and birds and birds rising higher and higher until they were carried out of sight and gone. I have never seen anything like that in my life. It was as if the birds were riding a wave, a swirl of energy that spiraled higher and wider until they were all we could see. I hadn't expected that even though, in retrospect, it was why we had come! Much to our surprise, we witnessed the vortex!

On our hike, I said to Steve, "We really don't have an old dog. She hasn't slowed down at all. She acted like this when I first got her from Ron eight years ago."

We had a great hike that day. It was picture perfect looking out across the Blue Ridge Mountains in all its ancient glory for hundreds of miles. At the top of Table Rock about 50 feet in front of us we saw a beautiful memorial with a cross and flowers set on a rock across a chasm just out of our reach. It was too dangerous for us to climb over for a closer look.

We wondered what had happened and closed our eyes for a moment of silence for whatever did and whoever had been so memorialized on that rocky precipice. By the feel of it, we knew we had borne witness to something special.

Meanwhile, Casey was running circles around us. She would lie down next to us panting with her signature smile revealing how happy she was. The three of us were content to be in the sun on top of a mountain on such a beautiful day. At the end of the day, however, I was the one who ended up with a fractured ankle…not Casey! I was on crutches, and despite her age, Casey was just fine.

The next day, though, I noticed a change in her behavior. She came up to me at my desk and nudged me. She wanted to go outside, so I let her out. Minutes later she wanted to come back in, so I let her back in; minutes later she wanted to go back out, so I let her out. Casey was not a fussy dog, so this behavior was abnormal. After two days of this same erratic behavior, I realized that she must be very uncomfortable. Maybe her tumor was more painful than we knew. Or maybe the hike shook something up in her.

I was busy working at my desk, and when she didn't scratch the door to come back in, I hobbled out on my crutches to check on her. I flew into a panic when I saw her! I threw my crutches aside and ran to her. She was standing in the yard with her tail between her legs, her head down, and her whole body shaking. I pulled her head up and looked into her eyes. They were glazed over, and I thought she'd had a stroke. I immediately called my friends to help me get her to the animal emergency room since I couldn't drive or lift her into the car with my broken foot. They were there in 10 minutes.

The time in the waiting room seemed endless even though it was only five minutes. My wonderful vet told me that she thought the tumor had metastasized to her brain causing a seizure. If it wasn't that, then Casey would recover. But Sarah explained that if she didn't recover, then I would have some tough decisions to make because she was not going to get better.

143

My heart dropped to the ground. I was battling a lump too big for my throat as my whole world turned upside down. I stared at the gray paint on the wall.

My Casey…

From that moment on, Casey never ate again. She would drink water and throw it up, so I had to give her less and less. We kept a heart-shaped clear crystal bowl full of water on the table near her and let her sip just a little so as not to get too sick. But her body rejected our offering every time. It broke my heart to have to take the bowl away while she was still lapping desperately—she was so thirsty! Over the next three days, she became weaker and weaker. I was so devastated that I dropped everything I was doing and devoted every minute to my dying dog, to my loyal companion who I never thought would leave my side.

I cannot tell you the long looks deep into her eyes and the longing in my heart. I would have given anything or done anything to save the life of my Casey. Everyone, including the vet, recommended I put her down, but I couldn't do it.

The next night, in the middle of the night, she came into my room and nudged me to take her outside. In our eight years together this was a first. She never got up in the middle of the night, not even once. She came back into the bedroom where she lay in my arms at the foot of the bed. She started into a rhythmic breathing pattern that I took as a sign she was starting to die. I gently petted her soft fur and thought she was going to die in my arms that night. I felt miraculously strong and somehow ready for it, but she didn't, and I held her until morning.

In the morning, I set her up on our couch since that was her favorite place to be and she was happy there. She loved lying on the couch, but we had always reserved that for special occasions and this definitely qualified. I wrapped a blanket around her, and she looked adorable with her little head coming out of the blanket. I was devastated to see her so lifeless.

My friend Kim came over, and we spent hours sobbing like babies watching sweet Casey decline. At one point she got off the couch and wobbled over to the chair and hunched behind it hugging the wall. I followed her and pulled the chair out and gave a long imploring look straight into her eyes. She reached out and licked my face in answer to my plea. She had tears in her eyes! Honestly, she did. She gave me several weak but heartfelt kisses. And then she licked my tears away! She wasn't staying this time. Her answer was clear.

That night Steve and I slept with our heads turned toward the foot end of the bed, so our heads were right next to Casey who was laying on the floor at that end of the bed. I laid awake with her all night as she struggled for her life. I must have fallen asleep around 4 AM when suddenly I got a nudge from her as she wobbled quickly past me with her little diaper on. I will never forget that image! She was so sweet!!! She was weak and wobbly and was heading straight for the wall! I jumped out of bed and caught her just in time to turn her around and help her out of the room. I placed her gently back on the couch.

That next day I received compassionate calls and visits from my friends begging me to put her down. But I couldn't do it. I struggled so hard with that concept! Who was I to decide that her life was over? I couldn't make that decision. I believe in the process of life. I feel we labor coming into this world and we labor going out, and I couldn't get myself to interfere with that.

We spent all day Sunday with Casey on the couch. She was

happy, we were happy, we watched football and movies and snuggled on the couch all day and all night and had the best day of our lives together, just the three of us. To see her that day you would never know that she was dying. She was smiling like she always did, that great big alligator smile, happy just to be with us! I could have stayed on that couch forever.

That night we camped in the living room. I slept on the couch with Casey and Steve slept on the floor in his sleeping bag. Casey's head lay on a sleeping bag on the couch, and I had a pillow scrunched under my head at the same height, and we looked deeply into each other's eyes all night long. It brought to mind the lyrics of the Pure Prairie League song, Boulder Skies, *"Take one long last look before I go."* It made me weep. I didn't sleep. I just lay there looking into the beautiful eyes of my dog, grateful to have her there with me, and grateful for having had her here for all these years. I prayed for her soul to return to me one day, knowing that a deal with God for more time was not going to happen.

About 3:00 in the morning I felt Casey wrestling to sit up, and she managed with effort to get herself up into a comfortable sitting position. I watched in stillness so as not to disturb her mission. I found her staring at the picture of Mother Meera, an Indian Avatar that I had placed on our coffee table, specifically to watch over Casey. She stared intently for about 20 minutes with that beautiful smile on her face.

I carefully, without creating any disturbance, reached for my iPad and took a picture. That photo now sits framed in my house.

Mother Meera is believed to be an embodiment of Divine Mother. She travels and meets with hundreds of people at a time, and gives her silent blessing of light and love by her sight and her touch to thousands of people throughout the world. Her devotees tell of many occasions where animals show up at her doorstep to die. Obviously, Mother's blessing was not bound by the framed photo, as Casey was receiving something very tangible during her silent, focused audience with the revered saint.

In the morning we resituated her comfortably on the couch with fresh towels and covered her with a fluffy blanket. She looked so sweet and peaceful. I noticed her eyes were receding. They were no longer of use on this earth. She was having a rough time keeping water down, so we almost stopped giving her water altogether. It was then that I realized we were "putting her down" by doing that. So I made some inquiring calls that morning.

I called a vet that specializes in animal euthanasia just to see if she was available, should I decide to let her go that way. Then I called the crematorium to have their information just in case it became relevant. I made it clear to them that this was only fact-finding, not a decision; it was only to get information, just in case. After that call, Casey had a little seizure. All my friends at this point strongly recommended that I put her down. I struggled. I still could not do it. Was I being compassionate? Was I being inhumane? Was I right? Was I wrong? Was I cruel? Was I selfish? I was a wreck. But I still felt—absolutely— that I could not put her down. A decision of that magnitude was not mine to make.

At this point, I looked at my sweet Casey and spoke to her out loud. I told her that I was going to go into the other room for a little while, and during that time she should just slip out of her body and take her last breath. I held her head and looked deeply into her beautiful eyes and thanked her for being such a loyal companion. I said everything I

147

wanted to say to her. Then I kissed her on the top of her head pressing my lips deep into her fur with raw emotion and all my love, tears streaming down my face. As I started to straighten up to leave, she put her paw on my arm and held me back. She did not want me to go. So I sat back down.

I petted her and petted her and looked deeply into her eyes and, while doing so, Steve surprised us by returning home for lunch. By this time she was having small seizures intermittently. I decided I needed more help with this decision. I called an animal communicator named Emerald. If Casey were to tell Emerald she wanted me to put her down, and if I believed Emerald was truly communicating with Casey, then I would do it. That is the only way I would do it.

After a few minutes, Emerald tuned into Casey and started relaying information that Casey wanted me to know. Immediately I knew it was Casey because Emerald was giving information that only Casey and I knew.

Through Emerald, we found out Casey's level of discomfort. I asked if she was in pain and she said that her head was tilted too much and told me how to place her head so she could breathe easier. I did that, and immediately her breathing eased. This gave me the confidence to continue with the session.

Casey relayed how much she was enjoying hearing the wind outside. It was a blizzardy day in Blowing Rock, and Emerald was in Pennsylvania, so I knew Casey was aware of her surroundings. She said she just wanted to close her eyes and rest and she did. Emerald went on to say what a strong and valiant girl Casey was. Casey told her she was experiencing much discomfort lately, but she was not a wimpy girl when it came to pain, and she was carrying on

148

so that she could be with us.

Now it was time for my big question, so I asked if she wanted us to put her down. Casey said we could put her down, and it would be easier for her, but only if it were easy for us, otherwise she would pass in a day or two on her own. She reiterated that I had to be OK with it. Specifically me. Then Casey asked what Steve thought about putting her down. She wanted his opinion because, as she put it, he is very balanced and she trusted him. (Emerald had not even heard of Steve at this point. Casey LOVED Steve! And he's a lawyer, and he IS very balanced and has solid, trustworthy opinions!)

She went on to say how much she loved me, that she's been so happy with me all these years. She said she loved looking at me "with deep eyes" as she put it. Casey and I always looked deeply into each other's eyes. From the moment I got her, I would stare into her eyes trying to see behind them, into her soul, to see "who" she was. She was not an ordinary dog. I always felt she was somehow human. I called her my "human dog." She told me that I was the coolest, best person in the world and that she loved me and had so much fun with me. She said she also loved Steve. She loved that I am a "live wire" and that Steve calmed her.

She explained how the right side of her neck was hot and burning and terribly uncomfortable. It would be easier for her to have help passing but if we decided not to do it she would make a go of it. She was very sad to leave us.

I asked her if she knew what caused the tumor and she said she thought it was the water. I asked her if there was anything she was unhappy about in her life with us and she said," I wish I could have been with you all the time, I mean ALL the time!" and she laughed knowing that was not possible. I asked her if she knew she was going to a better place and she laughed again, "Of course! You know the answer to that. You're so esoteric."

She then offered that she knew she had been the best friend in the world to me. She knew how much Steve loved her and how much Steve loved me. And she knew she would be alright and that she had done a good job as our dog.

It was all so poignant.

I asked her what her favorite things were and she said, "Just laying around with us and cuddling, and running around outside and of course, eating! She went on and on about how much she loved the outdoors and loved sitting on the earth. I have so many pictures of Casey on the lawn, in the flower beds, lying under the trees, content. "The earth," she said, "I love the earth."

On that note, we ended our conversation. Casey was tired and needed to rest.

I turned to Steve and asked him if he thought we should put her down. He said—for the first time—that he thought we should. "But" he added," only if you are 100% Ok with it because I don't want you to blame me down the road." I had total respect for that statement and decided against it, knowing that I wasn't ready and may have regrets down the line.

I'm sure that every dog owner can relate to my gut-wrenching dilemma. It's the same decision that people have to make about removing their loved ones from life support.

Casey and I were now in an equal struggle. She was struggling for her life; I was struggling with the decision to end her life. I read in some spiritual book once that we have a contracted number of breaths to take in this lifetime. If that is true then who am I to decide how many breaths

Casey should take and which one should be her last? I suppose if I decided to put her down then whatever breath became her last would have been the contracted number, and my decision would be part of that contract. If the contracted number of breaths is not true, then I still have the same question. This life or death dilemma brings up so many questions, moral, ethical, fate vs. free will. In the end, we can only do the best we can do according to our own awareness and conscience.

We sat in silence with our beautiful dog, savoring our final time together, knowing we had two days max according to Casey.

Minutes later, however, Casey erupted in a seizure that was SO BAD that I can't even talk about it. It was so horrific that I screamed! In that massive convulsion her eye sockets receded, her sight was gone, and she would never come back to us as Casey, and I knew it. She was gone for us as far as Casey was concerned. The seizure had besieged her already ravaged body yet she was still alive. My heart was jumping out of my chest in devastation. It was so horrible that I grabbed the phone and called the vet. I begged her to come; begged that Casey had to go as soon as possible. She said she would be there in an hour, at 3:30. I immediately turned to Steve, "I made the call." That way there would be no argument in the future.

Then I asked him to come over and sit with Casey and me. Suddenly we only had one remaining hour with our Casey. Steve held her legs so she could not hurt herself during any future seizures and I held her body tightly and talked to her in a low, soothing voice. Instantly there was a very noticeable change. Her breathing became loud and deep, guttural and rhythmic. Her back was arched, her head was stretched way back, and we could feel small seizures underneath our hold on her. I knew that this was the start of

151

her death. In an unaided death, that breathing could go on for many hours or even days and get fainter and fainter until the soul gently slips out of the body with the last breath. It's a gradual process out of the body and out of this life. Instead of that belabored time period I knew we only had one hour because the vet was on her way. We spoke softly and lovingly, encouraging our sweet Casey in her last moments.

After 30 minutes of this pattern, around 3 o'clock, I asked Steve what we should do with her body afterward. Our friend Debra had called earlier to offer her land as Casey's burial site so I would always know where she was. I appreciated the offer but didn't think I would take her up on that option. I planned to cremate her and have her with us sitting under her favorite tree and bringing her out to the lake with us and taking her to our cabin in Iowa. As we were discussing the possibilities, listening to her loud belabored breathing, the beginning of her two-day journey to her last breath, Steve looked up and with great insight said, "She just told us how much she loves the earth."

And with that word "earth"……absolute silence.

She was lifeless.

Our Casey was gone.

We sat in silence…in relief…in God's presence…and in Casey's.

Out of that reverent silence, Steve quietly spoke, "There's our answer." Casey was such an amazing communicator that she left on that word to let us know what she wanted. She loved the earth. There is so much to say about that moment. We were both shocked and relieved. We were barely breathing. She went from a rapidly breathing epileptic seizure posture to—instantly—like a magic trick—having her legs crossed lady-like, looking angelic with that big Casey smile and her enormous, enthusiastic energy charging out of her eyes.

When someone dies, their body remains in the position they were in when they died. I, to this moment, do not know how Casey got from her arched back and terrible epileptic position to this beautiful state of grace. That night Steve and I marveled at that fact and tried to understand how and when that happened.

Over the years I have come to realize that you can see a person's life in their face in death. Now I realized that even dogs have a face in death! Casey's highly charged, enthusiastic, eager spirit left its imprint on the cells of her body on its way out and left us with her happy, energetic, smiling face in death. It was beautiful beyond words. Her natural state of being. Stunning to witness.

It was only then that I knew my decision was right. It was extraordinary to see that beautiful Casey energy etched on her face. It is something we would not have seen if she had been put to sleep. We would have seen a peaceful sleeping dog but not the highly spirited, energetic, smiling face of Casey.

After her breathing and her heart so suddenly stopped, and we were sitting in utter shock, her heart started beating again!! I exclaimed, "She's breathing again! Look at my hand (which was over her heart) it's moving!" And then about 20 seconds later it stopped again…for good this time. Our baby was gone.

I knew that she went through all of that for me….so that I wouldn't have to put her down. She heard my conversations over the days and knew how strongly I felt about not being the one to make that determination. So she made sure I didn't have to. Once I made the call to the vet, on my own volition, after that terrible seizure, she knew that I had finally let go. So Casey knew that she could go. And she immediately started her exit and went into the death mode…the deep guttural breathing, a harbinger for the beginning of the process, which in her own words would be one or two days. And when Steve repeated Casey's words—how she loved the earth—she stopped breathing exactly on that word, so we would know to bury her at Debra's. Deep in the earth. She had spoken loud and clear.

We sat for a while, not even sad, just marveling at her beauty and all the energy flowing through that beautiful dog body of hers in the moments during and after her departure. We were high, relieved, and in tune with her soul. Her face in death reflected her whole life: energetic, excited, happy, loving and charged with enthusiasm. I have her beautiful face etched in my memory forever. Her face in death was so alive.

We called Debra and prepared to take Casey to her land. It was a blustery, COLD day and everyone was hunkered down for the storm that was coming to the east coast. Therefore we couldn't invite all of Casey's many friends to her spontaneous funeral. But I did call Cyndy who came with Nancy, and of course, Kim came, and we gathered at Debra's. The seven of us created a beautiful ceremony. Randy and Steve dug a purposely deep grave, and we arranged her blanket in the hole and lay her on it. I placed three of her favorite toys next to her. Then we went around the circle making wishes, and sprinkling this colorful confetti on her that Cyndy brought. Casey looked beautiful!! She sparkled with color, and I knew she loved it. She was such a blingy girl.

Then we went around the circle again saying something we appreciated about Casey and placing a flower over her heart. Some comments brought tears, and some brought laughter. Casey had so much personality and was so funny that we laughed remembering those endearing things about her. We bid her a fond and loving farewell. We hugged and cried and then it was time to go. It was cold outside, and the chill was now on the inside as well.

Steve and I had a solemn dinner with Debra and Randy, then drove home and made the dreaded walk through our front door into a deafly still and silent house—no tail wagging against the wall or pounding the floor in homecoming delight. Instead, our home felt cavernous and empty. Cold and silent. As I walked past the table where Casey's heart-shaped crystal bowl was still filled with water, it tipped over, spilling the remaining water on the carpet. I told Steve that I didn't touch it. I wasn't even that close to it. I didn't want to sound weird about everything now, but I knew I didn't do it. Casey did.

Later that night I told Steve he had never hugged me like that before. Because Casey would always wiggle between us and be inside our hug. We had never had a full-blown hug the whole time we'd been together. Ever.

The next morning I found myself paralyzed with grief. I couldn't get out of bed. The house was silent. It felt cold, and I was empty. I could not bear it. I made an appointment with Emerald to speak with Casey the next day.

The first thing Casey said to me was that she was fine. A wonderful tall woman who she liked was taking care of her. She reported that she was recuperating in what she described as a hospital, and she was out on the grounds resting outside, on the <u>earth</u> (!) Her caretakers were going to help her get her body back into its perfect state again. She had an inordinate amount of electricity in her body from the earth.

She said she saw me in bed grieving and then at my computer this morning; she saw me go into the kitchen feeling lost and wondering what to do, all of it was true. She knew how devastated I was and she wished she could do something and would try to figure out a way.

I asked her if she had seen Ron and she said Ron came running to her when she crossed over and that he was with her now. Eight years before this I inherited Casey from Ron. I asked her if she was coming back and she laughed and said, "I knew you were going to ask me that question!" She said she couldn't come back right away. She needed to rest and that it would take at least six months. Ron was beside her. He will send her with his blessings when it's time for her to come back. She will be a runner. She will be a small puppy coming toward me with great happiness, and her ears tipped over, with Shepherd markings.

I asked her how she liked the burial and she said she loved resting in the earth, she was glad the grave was so deep. She liked there were more people there and that it was casual and not completely sad. She liked something I put in her grave very much. Emerald was trying to see exactly what it was; not a ball but something she played with. I told her it was her favorite toy and Emerald said "more than one," and I confirmed there were three. She then said that Casey was showing her something else, but Emerald could not determine what it was, but it was very colorful. She kept saying," I just can't tell what that is but it's full of different colors. It's sparkly" I told her about the confetti, and then Casey told Emerald that she loved the confetti!

I asked Casey to describe her experience of leaving her body. She said that my call to the vet gave her a surge of energy. Before the call, she was worried she didn't have enough energy to pass on. But my call gave her relief and renewed energy to go right away—and then she was on her way. She explained that she was in a dark tunnel for quite awhile. She started to give up and was feeling lost but then she was aware that we were there and that she was alright. She then gathered more energy, and she "got there" by moving toward and into the light. She felt out of breath when Ron came running to meet her. She said it was easy once she left her body. She came back into her body again and then she shot out for good. It was dark at first, but she knew where to run. She ran into the light and then she was out of her body and free.

Now…having heard her experience, let me tell you my side of this. She had said earlier in the day (the day she died when she spoke through Emerald) that she would pass naturally in a day or two. I felt she had two more days and she was going to pass on Halloween, the same day my brother passed. I just felt that. When I made the call to the vet, her soul knew that I was finally OK with letting her go, I finally had accepted it. That gave her relief and also energized her. So she went for it.

She passed on before the vet came so I wouldn't have to put her down. She heard all of my conversations with my friends; she knew how much I did NOT want to do that. I wanted her to go of her own accord and not take her life away from her before her time. She did not want me to have to live with that.

So after my determined call to the vet, she willed herself out of her body in a very intensive 30-minute process that would have naturally taken one or two days to complete. And because of that—because she willed herself to go

157

NOW and had to push herself extraordinarily to do it—
because she condensed a process that normally takes two
days into 30 minutes—she went into darkness first before
coming into the light. I think she came back into her body
for 20 seconds to get her last wind to make her final surge.

Death is a process, and she had one or two days of
processing left to go. In a normal situation, one starts that
labored breathing and the breathing becomes less and less
over many hours or many days until the breathing becomes
shallow and stops. During that time you are processing
your spirit out of the body and then, fully processed, the
spirit, with a wisp, soars out of the body with the last breath
into the light.

It's like when you bleed, and it forms a scab, the scab pulls
away from the skin as the skin heals. Once the skin is all
healed the scab naturally falls off and doesn't leave a scar.
It just peels away and falls off. So too with the spirit. It
processes itself away from the body and its life on earth,
detaches itself little by little, and one day naturally slips
effortlessly away.

If Casey had not chosen to leave her body so abruptly, the
additional couple of days would have allowed her spirit to
more gradually prepare for its detachment. Little by little
she would have detached and then with her last breath she
would have soared effortlessly from her body—straight
into the light.

But because she willed her spirit out ahead of the normally
scheduled time, and chose to speed up the process, she
went into a dark tunnel. But even though it was dark, she
knew where she was going. She knew where to run. And
she ran into the light and was met by Ron. It's amazing,
isn't it? I was so grateful to have this information about the
details of Casey's death.

I asked her if she knew we were there with her and she said she was out of it, but she could smell us still, and it was comforting. She carries our scent with her even now. She said she wished she could squeeze between us when we hug!

Then I asked her if we had been together in a past life. She showed Emerald pictures of two sisters holding hands, about the same size, slender, graceful women. She said we were sisters in love, she saw us in the woods holding hands, and we loved each other, and we were human. It was an idyllic setting many lifetimes back. When she met me this lifetime, she knew who I was, and she loved me. As a side note, Ron would always say, "Casey really loves you!" And I would respond to him by saying, "Casey loves everyone!" And he would respond, "No. With you it's different."

Casey went on to say that she will be able to visit us. She's on the floor right now in her place, and she can knock things over. Emerald didn't understand that, but I did! She said she knocked the heart bowl over. She described in detail all the many ways we played together and how much fun she had. I asked her what her howl meant every time we walked in the door, and every time friends came over, and she said it was," Yippee Hooray! Yay Yay Yay!"

I asked her about swimming since she LOVED to swim any chance she got. She said she loved the feel of water on her skin. It was a glorious feeling on her skin. Then she showed Emerald a picture of a dolphin...so perhaps a past life of Casey? Who knows?

I asked her about my friend Kim's dog Eros. Casey said she and Eros would run around together and she liked him very much. He was a cool dog. But she said she had to boss him around a bit and put him in his place because she wasn't a puppy like him and he needed to be less rough with her. He complied with her wishes. It was fun to hear about the communication between the dogs.

As a joke, I asked Casey if she liked rice. Emerald responded by saying she was sure I wanted her to say yes it was her favorite food, but she was not getting that answer from Casey. In fact, Casey was staring at her bowl and saying, "Whaaaat?" No, she didn't like rice, Casey said. When Casey got her tumor, Steve would cook chicken with rice for her. I used to tell Steve that Casey would never eat the rice. But he insisted on making her fresh rice saying it was good for her. I told him I didn't think animals in the wild ate their meat and then thought: "Now we must find some rice to balance our meal!" I just didn't think it worked that way. In fact, Casey many times took her bowl and turned it upside down on the floor when there was just rice left in it!! She was a clear communicator!

One time she took her bowl of dry food and turned it upside down on the floor. She then proceeded to eat the big chunks and left the little chunks on the floor. That's when I started feeding her big chunk dog food.

I asked her if there was anything else she wanted to say to me. She said she feels my love and it's nice to be in the light of my love. She said when we were young women together she loved that she could hug me, and it's the only thing in this life together that she missed, otherwise it was a blast!

With that, the conversation was over. She was doing fine. I was relieved to know that. Only I wasn't doing fine now, and she wanted to help me with that.

After many days of deep grieving, I found the quote by Maharishi about grief that I referred to in an earlier story:

Grief is natural. At first, when grief is deep and sharp, these emotions allow the soul to feel that they were deeply loved. It is also natural that the grieving should taper off, allowing the soul to feel that their passing was not a drag on the life of their beloved ones and that they are free to move on to their Destiny. It is important to feel positivity and support for the departed soul wherever they may be because our attitude affects their evolution.

I needed to find help with my grief. To find a way to go on living without the unconditional love of my beloved companion. I found a renowned healer from Australia who took the pain out of my broken heart within minutes and also out of my fractured foot. I felt renewed. I never imagined what the loss of unconditional love would feel like. It's not something we experience very often in life since human love is conditional.

I thought back to our hike at Table Rock. In my mind, I saw the cross and flower memorial and wondered if it was really there or if it rose for our eyes only, as a premonition. I walked the 50-foot chasm to the memorial. I sat in silence, now knowing the grief and the loss that the cross and flowers represented. I sat in silent prayer for the grieving and the grieved.

Ohhhhh Casey…you were only on loan to us. We had to give you back. In the end, everything is like library books. You can enjoy them for a while, but then you have to give them back. With deepest gratitude, we gave you back. You are the sweetest story in the whole collection.

My hope is also my knowing that our darkest moments bring the brightest light. And perhaps I will find that little puppy running to me with ears tipped forward, Shepherd markings, howling "Yippee Hooray!" And jumping back into my arms once again. I look forward to that. I look for that everywhere I go, in every dog I see. My arms are open wide, and my heart even wider. In this lifetime or another, they will always be open and waiting for my Casey.

A MESSAGE IN THE CASKET

~ I delivered the following eulogy from Blowing Rock,
North Carolina, speaking into the phone which broadcast
my voice into a microphone at Steve's funeral~

February 25, 2012, Eau Claire Wisconsin

Eulogy for Steve

*So one day Steve just got into his car and drove himself to
the VA hospital and lay down in bed and gradually made a
transition out of his body and out of this world. With hardly
a word to anyone, without a warning of what was to come,
he simply got in his car and drove. We have nine months on
the other end of our lives to make the transition **into** this
body. We take this **immense light** that we are, and squeeze
it into these little tiny itsy bitsy bodies and scream all the
way into this world. We spend years getting comfortable in
it, and somewhere in the middle feel normal and adjusted
and pretty good. Until one day the light inside us is just too
big to fit into this body anymore. And so, that day we get in
our car and drive ourselves to the hospital and lay down in
bed and make our transition out of this world and back into
that **amazing light** that we are.*

For those of us left behind, our tapestry has changed. There

163

was a particular color of thread that had woven itself into the fabric of our lives that we won't see again. That thread, however, is as vibrant on the other side of the tapestry and others marvel at the new beautiful color that they suddenly see. Everyone on THAT side of the tapestry is rejoicing! It's just that we, on this side, can no longer see it.

And so it is—with such deep sadness—that I mourn the loss of my oldest friend, my neighbor, and my steadfast friend throughout all the years of my life. No one on this planet outside of my family has known me longer than Steve. We grew up together. He was the only boy at all my birthday parties every single year! We beat a path between each other's houses, and we would walk the path to each other's house every day as kids.

I went to college with Steve, and we partied like crazy people, Litch and Lenny...that's what we called each other. I have hundreds of memories of Steve in college, and each one is bursting with FUN! Steve was always upbeat, friendly and hyper-ly funny! He lit up a room! Then we went our separate ways with infrequent visits here and there throughout the rest of our lives.

At one point I was living in Port Angeles, Washington, and was broke. Steve, who lived many hours away, surprised me by careening through my front door with HUGE bags of groceries! "Lenny, I've got something for you!" He was such a generous friend! I hadn't seen him in years, and he barges in with groceries.

I last saw him in Chetek Wisconsin in 2010 at a reunion with my brothers and their wives and... once again...Litch and Lenny! We were at Gilligan's Tiki Bar where I took a picture of the tablecloth because I wanted to replicate it for my place on Watauga Lake aptly named MargOritaville. The tablecloth was colorfully designed with palm trees and

*flamingos and flip-flops. Steve couldn't believe I was taking
a picture of a tablecloth—without people in it—so he put
his face on the table so there would be a person in the
picture! Then Marty and Carmen followed suit, and
suddenly everybody had their heads on the table! It was a
typical zany Steve moment which became absolutely
hysterical! We laughed so hard that the people around us
started to laugh and the whole tiki bar was drawn into our
scene. We had a great time that day! I am left with that
memory vividly ingrained in my heart....the memory of fun-
loving, funny, hyperly happy Steve.*

*We went through a lifetime together, through all the joys,
and all too many sorrows and everything in between.*

*But Steve, you were only on loan to us. We were blessed by
your generous soul, your happy spirit, your great big light-
up-the-room smile, your contagious laugh and your funny,
zany sense of humor. You were a beautiful, delightful gift
and a genuine friend to us all. You take my heart with you
wherever you go, my dear friend. You take all of our hearts
with you. You are deeply loved and will be deeply missed,
but....I assure you.....we will "walk the path" once again,
on the other side of the tapestry, when we meet again
somewhere in this amazing, mysterious, glorious universe.*

I love you, Steve Litchfield. I wish you the light of God.

~Later that day my brother texted me a picture of the room
with all the flowers surrounding Steve in his casket~ and
these were my thoughts:

If I had actually been at Steve's funeral, I would have done
something completely different. Had I seen the red

Hawaiian shirt that draped his body in the casket in the middle of a Midwestern winter, I would have changed my whole approach to the eulogy. It was only then, for the first time, that I saw Steve and his lifetime clearly. His red shirt told his whole story.

He studied physics because he wanted to understand himself. Now I understood him.

Steve was a specific type of catalyst. Whenever he came into a room, he created a chemical reaction that turned any normal situation into chaos...electric, highly charged, very fun chaos. He was a hyper fireball of energy, and he added that element to whatever was happening. If you were already having fun, it would become chaotic fun. That day at the Tiki Bar when he put his face on the table, and we all followed suit, the whole scene went from normal to chaotic in seconds! Everyone had their heads on the table, and even the people next to us started to join in as the chemical reaction grew—and it became hysterical, sparked by Steve.

That was his thing. He always created wild chemical reactions.

When I saw the red Hawaiian shirt, I realized all of this. Steve walked into any room, and the chemistry abruptly changed. I am sure that his purpose on earth was to help people realize their potential for extreme fun and to remind us to have a good time and not take things so seriously. He lay there in that shirt to give us one final reminder!

We should all be so self-realized to wear a red Hawaiian shirt to our own funeral. Steve was done here. He was on to the next gig and ready to party, and he left his message in his casket:

Let go of everything everyone has told you about what to do or how to be. Just be yourself. Don't conform to anyone else's style or doctrine. Live your truth in the way in which you were created. You will find that your greatest joy comes from being yourself.

Each one of us is different. Like snowflakes, we fell out of the sky in different patterns and came together for this short period of time we call "our life." In another short time, every one of these snowflakes here today will melt. It's a changing universe, meant to be that way, always will be that way. So be yourself while you are here. You are here to be unique, wonderful YOU. So be that. This is what he came to tell you.

Let him be an example of that for you.

If I had actually been at the funeral, we would have had a standing ovation for Steve for being himself in death as well as in life. We would have stood and applauded his red Hawaiian shirt! It would have turned into a revival because Steve was there and he would have created one last chemical reaction that would have turned his funeral into wild hysteria! We would have been lifted to our feet by the sheer joy of his life.

This is what it's all about!

You don't and can't always "see" someone while they are alive because you are in your body and they are in theirs, and there are issues that mask the underlying Truth of each soul. There is no clear channel of vision when we are all caught up in our lives. When someone dies everyone around them is forced to stop. We are shocked into stopping and "seeing" that person for who and what they truly are. Now they are gone, and we have stopped to appreciate them; nothing stands in our way of seeing them. We can settle into their essence and finally know them.

With nothing in the way, we appreciate their soul with a new depth and clarity.

When someone dies, it's the only time we truly reflect on ONLY THAT PERSON. Regardless of how we saw them in life, regardless of what we thought of them, regardless of our relationship with them, our vision is clear once they leave their body. Only then can we see them, and we see them for a reason—we learn something from how they were in their life. It is their parting gift to us. Their entire life adds up to their moment of death that we see in their face at that point of passing over. Their essence at that moment is their gift to us. Simultaneously, it is our opportunity to accept them and finally appreciate them, and keep their essence living within us. A part of them becomes us, and that is the great gift of death. There is a reason we have funerals.

So, I just saw Steve today. I appreciated him yesterday, but I saw him today.

After this funeral—today—everyone needs to go shopping—and find their version of the red Hawaiian shirt. Wear that "shirt" proudly every day of your life! And make every day of your life a celebration and a reflection of unique and beautiful YOU in the exact way in which you were created.

A CLEAR VOICE

Okay, it's time to get our brooms out!

There is one person who I haven't mentioned in these memoirs that should be. My mother's older sister, Janet who I loved both because she was so much like my mother and also because she was so different. She was a beautiful, gracious socialite, but unlike my mother, she didn't drink. At all. She was a Christian Scientist and lived by very strict religious mores. When my mother died, she became my mother figure to some extent, but not entirely since she lived two hours away in Minneapolis.

I saw the best of life in her. She seemed to have room in her heart for everyone. I nicknamed her "The Walking Heart." I made a Valentine card for her one year that was simply a big red heart with legs and her name on it. She was ever busy, hosting parties, family holidays, and summer gatherings with boat rides at their house on Lake Minnetonka. She was always so eager about her endeavors, and I can still hear her exuberant, raspy Norwegian laugh.

We were close to this side of the family because my mother and her sister Janet married my father and his brother, Pierre. Two sisters marrying two brothers made the cousins extra close and the similarities pretty astounding. We were all rebellious. We rebelled against our mother's alcoholism; they rebelled against their parent's strict prohibitions. When they came to our house in Eau Claire, they would sneak outside with my brothers to smoke or drink or do whatever they could get away with.

As Janet and I got to know each other as adults, we found we shared similar beliefs about life and God. So much so that she said I was about an inch away from being a Christian Scientist. Therefore she never pushed her religion on me. She came to realize that I was an ardent student of life, finding my own way, and ending up close to her beliefs anyway...just without the rules.

She knew I was comfortable with my relationship to God and that I didn't feel the need to conform to any religion although I respected that she did. We had tremendous acceptance of each other's beliefs. She respected my choice to live according to my heart. I respected her choice to live according to Mary Baker Eddy.

Before she died, I flew to Minneapolis to see her one last time. She was bedridden and had developed dementia. Even so, I spent lovely hours with her reminiscing her life, hearing stories about my mom and dad when they first met, and other family stories. My cousins had warned me that she might not know who I am and wouldn't be able to carry on a conversation with me. But amazingly, every time I asked her a question she went deep into the answer with great clarity. When the memory was over, she would fade out, and I'd let her rest. Then I'd ask her another question, and deep into the story she went!

After spending an afternoon by her side, listening to her interesting stories, we were down to snippets of conversation as she faded in and out of awareness. She was peacefully falling asleep when suddenly she woke up, grabbed my hand, and looked me straight in the eyes. In a surprisingly coherent voice, she uttered her final words to me, "Stay on your path and keep it swept."

Those words resound in me. Be myself, travel to the beat of my unique drum, stay on MY path but keep it clean as I go. Tidy up! Resolve things, forgive, live with integrity. Be nice. Create good feelings. And, like her, be gracious.

I thought of a poster I saw in a doctor's waiting room:" Be kind, for everyone you meet is fighting a battle you know nothing about."

I strive to remember that. To live with that awareness.

I try to sweep up every day, so my life is simple and loving and straightforward, free of unresolved issues, honest and simple. And with a knowing that we are all fighting our own battles.

People talk about being on a spiritual path, or a religious path to God. But the truth is, our life is our path, spiritual, religious or otherwise.

We need to live our life with integrity with who we are; change our life as we change within ourselves; grow and become more true to our self every day, but keep it tidy as we go. Clean it up. Keep it clean. Beat our drum. And keep sweeping.

I consciously do that. I keep an awareness of the battle someone may be going through. I feel it in my heart. And I am never truer to myself as when I extend an unspoken understanding and compassion to everyone I meet. It is not an easy discipline but an important one. Stay aware of it, keep this in the back of your mind, and you will see your behavior and your life improve.

Get out your broom. Sweep your sidewalks.

Every day.

Stay on your path. And keep it swept.

THE MEDICINE BAG

They couldn't find Charlie's medicine bag, so I gave him mine.

"Of course you should give him your medicine bag," said my friend Debra who had taken me on the Shamanic journey to see my brother. "You were good medicine for Charlie."

There are moments in your life that you are born for. This was one of them.

Though born a white American, Charlie's beliefs were mainly focused around two traditions of knowledge, the Vedic knowledge from India and traditional Native American. Both have a commonality in that they honor the laws of nature, respect the four directions, the earth elements, and the four seasons.

When Charlie died, he left very clear instructions about how he wanted to be buried. In a casket above ground with his rudraksha beads, his knife, and his medicine bag. Rudraksha beads from the eastern tradition and the rest from the Native American tradition. Everything was granted. Everything came together easily by going to his cabin in the woods. But the only thing they couldn't find was his medicine bag. It's because I had it.

Here begins my story of Charlie, my deepest connection on this planet outside of my own family. He was our tribe. My brothers were his brothers. He was my heart, and I knew him completely. I understood him. Charlie. My love. My friend.

I cannot go into the whole story of Charlie in this book because he was unique and it would require volumes. In summary, he was very authentic in the way he lived his life. He lived relentlessly and uncompromisingly according to his values, and it was unconventional indeed. Any encounter with Charlie would be memorable.

Charlie was a lover of the outdoors. A cross-country runner, he also ran the Boston marathon. A lover of the wind and the water, he was a competitive sailor at the Mendota Yacht Club in Madison. He spent much of his time camping and canoeing in the solitude of the Boundary Waters in northern Minnesota made up of rugged cliffs, and canyons, and rock formations left behind by the glaciers. He had a strong affinity for Lake Superior, its depth, and clear, clean, cold water. He was happiest on the lakes deep in the northern forests.

After college Charlie became a teacher of Transcendental Meditation and traveled Wisconsin giving lectures and teaching. I helped him set up his class in Oshkosh which is where our relationship began. He left for Switzerland to study Vedic Science at Maharishi European Research University (MERU), and when he returned to Madison, I joined him there for several years. Within six months of our break up, we were both married to other people but maintained a deep friendship throughout all the years of his life.

Charlie grew up well-off, but his drum beat differently than the rest of his family. I think it's fair to say it beat differently than the rest of most people. For example, while living at his family home, he never understood why his mother was upset when he tossed out his mattress and pounded railroad ties into the super expensive wallpaper in his bedroom so he could hang up a hammock to sleep in. I had to mediate that incident which, it turns out, was the first of many. I spent countless evenings negotiating with his mother while trying to stay true to Charlie.

I once made a bet with him, and I lost. What was at stake for the winner was 10 wool Hudson Bay blankets. There was originally only one blanket at stake, but because I was so certain I was right I upped the ante to 10! I even threw in a hammock. When I learned how wrong I was, Charlie was pretty excited about getting 10 wool blankets. And because I pay my debts but I couldn't afford 10 blankets, I had to figure out how to repay him. So, unbeknownst to him, I borrowed a loom and bought beautiful natural-colored, textured wool yarn and wove him a blanket. I had never woven anything before so had to learn from scratch. I even spun my hair into yarn and wove it into the blanket at the point where the blanket would cover his heart. Many months later, long after he forgot about the debt, never expecting payment for it, I gifted him with my masterpiece. He was pretty darn moved. In fact, he was speechless for quite awhile.

He was great friends with a Native American medicine man, Chief Wilbur Blackburn, who Charlie often visited in his home in Black River Falls. Wilbur was one of Charlie's most esteemed friends. I visited Wilbur with Charlie on several occasions. They loved each other deeply and felt a bond of trust and shared like-mindedness. Wilbur was always giving Charlie gifts, so perhaps he was the one who gave him his medicine bag although I don't know that for sure. If he did, it would be his most cherished item. We visited him after a fire burned thousands of acres in Black River Falls. The police came to Wilbur's house with orders to evacuate, but he instead, confidently, stayed in his home, honoring the sacred fire. It came within 30 feet of his home when the fire split in two and went right around his property. He took us outside to show us the incredible, might I say, the miraculous course of the fire.

Charlie's was a life of extremes, from a silent transcendental life with a living master in Switzerland to the dregs of the world. He spent many years with Maharishi Mahesh Yogi, the teacher of Transcendental Meditation in deep silence in Switzerland. Then he earned a Masters degree in Fine Arts from the University of Wisconsin in Madison. An artist, he dealt in pottery and antiques, but later in scrap metal and rough-hewn homes built by his own once-refined hands. His latter homes lacked running water because he liked to shower outside and use compost toilets. He had such refinement on the one hand but was rough and tough on the other.

His philosophy can be summed up in something he once said to me, "If you lose touch with the ditch you've lost touch with life."

He said the ditch keeps you real. Your life can be all fat and happy, but without the ditch, you do not keep a proper perspective on life. It keeps you real. There is good in life, and there's bad in life, and the whole gamut in between, but the ditch keeps you grounded in the full reality. No matter how good it gets, there's still the ditch.

When I lost Charlie, I gained the entire picture of our life. I said in an earlier chapter that truth has a way of letting you know it is true. Well here is the truth.

I was given a medicine bag years ago during a pipe ceremony. I have kept it in a safe place ever since. When Charlie died, I brought that medicine bag out and put it near my bed to feel close to him. When they searched his cabin for the items with which he wanted to be buried, they couldn't find his medicine bag, so they emailed me for help. Debra told me to give him mine; that I was good medicine for Charlie, but to put a personal item of mine in the bag. She said I would be drawn to the right item. Within minutes I had the perfect item, blessed it and put it in the bag. I looked at Charlie's photo on my desk, and his smile started laughing. His smile was so bright that it laughed and I laughed too with tears streaming down my face. My heart filled with the most indescribable love, and I knew at that moment that I was born to provide his medicine bag when he crossed over.

It created a feeling within me beyond words. It was HIS medicine bag, and I knew it, and he knew it, and he was happy and laughing. He knew all along that I had his medicine bag. Now I'm not even sure he ever had one. If he did, then this is the one he was supposed to take with him. That's why they couldn't find his.

Filling it gave a purpose and direction to my grief. It connected me to the people he loved the most on this earth. Now I have a bond with his family and friends who, until now, were total strangers to me. It also exposed me to his spiritual beliefs which have enriched my own tremendously.

It made me think about the concept of how people in other cultures bury things with them, like the Pharaohs in Egypt, which I never really understood since you can't take it with you. Charlie did the same but in a Native American manner.

Everything that people bury with them is symbolic of their beliefs and what was important in their life. The medicine bag is the same thing. It is filled with important symbolic items from your life as well as tobacco, cedar, sweet grass, sage and whatever else might be significant to the person.

I thought deeply about the medicine bag.

We need to send our loved ones off with a proper medicine bag. It should represent everything that was important to that person and everything that you wish for them, the deep intentions in your heart. That is the point of a funeral, that is the point of grieving, and that is the point of remembering all that we feel for that person.

The point is we have a medicine bag in our heart that belongs to the people that we love and we fill that bag as we share our life with them. Fill it with good medicine. Nonjudgmental acceptance, understanding, love, support and all good things. When they leave us, we need to send that with them, with all of our love and our very best wishes so their spirit can soar.

I was good medicine for Charlie, so I got to be the keeper and the provider of his medicine bag. I sent it off with pure intentions for a full and magnificent next life based on his interests and loves from this life. I was born to do that.

We need to be good medicine for each other during our life. We need to honor each other's lives. Then we need to honor each other's wishes in death and send each other off in the highest and most sacred manner. In that way, we help them on their journey, and it makes our grieving easier. It brings us together in honoring them, and it generates great purpose.

The medicine bag is holy.

Fill it with love.

While grieving Charlie, walking through my days, performing my tasks, and feeling the deep sorrow in my heart, I felt closer to God than I've ever felt. My grief became the most beautiful part of me. I let it be. I was walking through Staples in my jeans and no makeup and barely combed hair on a rainy Sunday afternoon, and a lovely glowy feeling came over me. A glow similar to that of being in love but a different, deeper, flavor. Feeling my pain enhanced me like nothing else because the pain of loss is the deepest emotion we will ever feel. It is closest to the source of all emotion. It is closest to The Creator. The pain in my heart brought me directly to God, and I knew it would eventually transform into an equal amount of joy, and Charlie would live within me. It is part of our sacred journey of life and love and loss and new life. It lifted me and shifted my perspective.

And brought light to my mourning.

THE REVIEW BOOTH

When we get to the end of our life and sit in our little "review booth" with God and evaluate our life, I'll be grateful to these people for the lessons I've learned.

My Father: *Keep your heart open in love through all things. Your final moment will add up to all of your choices you made at every moment.*

Ryan: *People do not die. They transform. It is a continuum of life.*

My Mother: *Living with regret is the greatest pain of death. Resolve everything before it's too late or it will haunt you after they die.*

Mike: *It's not as important who you are with as how you are behaving with whomever you are with. It's about you and how you live your moments.*

Tom: *There is plenty for everyone in this world, and that's the miracle!*

Casey: *Animals are magnificent creatures who are sensitively aware of what's going on and communicate with us. They have their own death journey and are acutely aware of it. I look deeply into their eyes and see their soul.*

Litch: *Be your unique self. God created you exactly how he or she wanted you to be. So be that.*

Auntie Janet: *Live with integrity on your life path and keep your path swept.*

Charlie: *Be good medicine for everyone and everything. Life is sacred; treat it with appreciation and reverence.*

GOOD GRIEF!

Grieving the loss of loved ones are moments we wish we didn't have to go through. But it 's these very experiences that become the most important moments in our life.

When someone comes into this world we rejoice, and when they leave we celebrate them; but before we can celebrate we have to grieve. Truly and deeply.

Grieving is really important. We need to do it. We need to go through it. Don't hold the tears back and "be strong." That is not grieving. Cry until the tears are gone. Open your heart and surrender to it. You need to express the grief you feel as you feel it. You'll make it through it, but you have to go through it. It will lessen and eventually turn to joy, but meanwhile, you have to take the time to grieve. It's one of the most important processes you will ever go through.

Never are we more authentic than when our heart is broken open in raw grief; never are we more integrated in body, mind, and emotion; and never are we in a more genuine place of love.

When someone dies we find ourselves staring off, intentionally trying to see them in our mind as we remember a specific moment when we were with them; we try to hear their voice, their laugh, what they said the last time we spoke. As we do this, we simultaneously metabolize them into our heart. We remember something about them, we grieve that memory, and then another one comes up, and we grieve that. As we remember memories, we incorporate them into our heart. Then we remember again, we grieve, and we incorporate that. And this goes on and on until the grieving subsides.

Once they are fully within us, the grieving becomes less because they are established in our heart; everything is reorganized—in our heart—and they are alive in us.

This is the process of opening to grief, integrating it and stabilizing our loved ones within us. We tuck them deep into our heart and continue our relationship with them.

Their memory is our connection to eternity, our connection to the divine, our connection to them. They never leave us even though we let them go. The depth of our grief becomes the depth of the joy we feel on the other side of the grief. It is a direct gift from them—our reward for loving them so deeply. They opened our heart, and their absence has created a big empty cavity. But this eventually fills back up with an equal amount of joy, and allows us to love more deeply than we have ever loved before.

So you see…it's a really big important process. This is the purpose of grieving. This brings light to your mourning.

I leave you with this quote from Maharishi from an earlier chapter because it's important to remember:

> *Grief is natural. At first, when grief is deep and sharp, these emotions allow the soul to feel that they were deeply loved. It is also natural that the grieving should taper off, allowing the soul to feel that their passing was not a drag on the life of their beloved ones and that they are free to move on to their Destiny. It is important to feel positivity and support for the departed soul wherever they may be because our attitude affects their evolution.*

184

EPILOGUE

I live by these messages.

These people guide me. I wondered where they went…they just disappeared.

Well—they didn't! They are bigger than ever. They flash big beacons of light and guide my everyday life; they echo within me and keep me on my highest path. In challenging times they shine even brighter. They become laser lights helping me thread the eye of the needle.

If there is one thing I have learned from these difficult losses it's that there is a silver lining in everything. Out of the ashes comes new life. In my darkest moments, I can flip a switch and see the bright soul of my brother shining through the light bulb with that impish grin on his face and know the truth of life. "I didn't die."

ABOUT THE AUTHOR

 Margo received a degree in Journalism from the University of Wisconsin in Oshkosh. She has journeyed far from her Midwestern roots to live a fulfilling life in service of others. She has taught meditation and stress management in major U.S. corporations, as well as in Egypt, India, the Philippines, Czech Republic and Slovakia. Before alternative medicine was in vogue, she started and managed an Ayurveda health center in Palm Beach, Florida.

Her varying interests have run the gamut from relationship coaching to officiating weddings to managing a rock band. She has been a Realtor for the past 21 years in Blowing Rock and Boone, North Carolina where she currently resides.